RANDALL
& HOPKIRK deceased

Also published by Boxtree:

STINGRAY
THUNDERBIRDS ARE GO!
CAPTAIN SCARLET
UFO & SPACE 1999

RANDALL & HOPKIRK deceased

GEOFF TIBBALLS

With a Foreword by Kenneth Cope

ITC.

BOXTREE

First published in Great Britain in 1994 by Boxtree Limited,
Broadwall House, 21 Broadwall, London SE1 9PL

1 3 5 7 9 10 8 6 4 2

ISBN: 0 7522 0915 9

Designed and typeset by Blackjacks, London

Printed and bound in Belgium by Proost International Book Production

A CIP catalogue entry for this book is available from the British Library.

Contents

Acknowledgements

The author would like to thank the following for their invaluable help in the preparation of this book: Kenneth Cope, Annette André, Monty Berman, Gerald Kelsey, Alf Joint, Vanessa Bergman of the *Randall & Hopkirk (Deceased)* Appreciation Society, Andrew Pixley, Tony McKay, Michael Richardson, Time Screen – the excellent magazine of British Telefantasy, Keith Richmond, Hilary Kingsley, Jon Keeble at ITC, Jack and Jonathan at Blackjacks and Boxtree editor Krystyna Zukowska.

Introduction

Marty Hopkirk returns to the office of 'Randall & Hopkirk – Private Investigators', full of a case he has taken over from his partner Jeff Randall. Before he has a chance to convey his thoughts to Jeff, Marty's loving wife Jean rings to find out when he is likely to be home. Taking the hint, Marty drives back to their flat but, in the course of crossing the road, is knocked down and killed by a hit and run driver. Far from being the end of the partnership, the spirit of Marty returns as television's first ghost detective. The office door now reads: 'Randall & Hopkirk (deceased)'.

Like many series before and after, *Randall & Hopkirk (deceased)* was not an immediate success. But remember how *Monty Python's Flying Circus* initially seemed to go out at a time just after the little dot disappeared from the screen, its erratic scheduling being interrupted by such compulsive viewing as the *Horse of the Year Show* – or how a critic wrote of the first episode of *Coronation Street*: 'The programme is doomed...with its dreary signature tune and grim scene of a row of terraced houses and smoking chimneys.' Thus it was with *Randall & Hopkirk*. There was a feeling that, in dealing with death in a somewhat frivolous manner, it was treading on new, dangerous and even hallowed ground. There were internal disputes over the direction the series should take. Some ITV regions did not show all 26 episodes.

Yet 25 years on, *Randall & Hopkirk (deceased)* is more popular than ever. It has finally been recognised as a classic programme of its time, with its humour lifting it above most of its contemporaries. It has developed a cult following with its own enthusiastic appreciation society. Now with the re-runs on BBC2 plus video releases, it is set to win a whole new army of fans.

And anyway what's wrong with having a ghost on your side? Think how useful an apparition would be for scattering the queue at the Post Office or for spooking all the supermarket trolleys to steer into each other so that they end up in an undignified heap. Come to think of it, perhaps Marty's haunting Sainsbury's already...

Geoff Tibballs

Foreword
By Kenneth Cope

Picture the scene. I was sitting at home having had a lot of success in *That Was The Week That Was* and as Jed Stone in *Coronation Street* when the phone rang and it was casting director Bob Leonard. He said: 'Kenny, we want you to star in a series – you get killed in the first episode!' I reckon he must have waited all his life to say that...

And so I came to play Marty Hopkirk. I had died in quite a few things – often the result of dodgy scripts – but this was my first shot at a ghost. It was a great series to make, the crew were terrific and Michael and Annette were such lovely people to work with. At the time, we knew it was good – it was a big mistake not to make a second series – but who would

have thought it would still be so popular nearly 25 years on? Even now, I still get asked, 'Where's your white suit, Marty?' and 'How did you disappear?'

My personal theory as to why *Randall & Hopkirk* (people sometimes used to get the name wrong – Michael and I called it 'Marshall & Snellgrove Diseased') has stood the test of time is that it harks back to nicer days when the sun shone. The sun always seemed to be shining whenever I went to the studio. Also, the show was innocent. There's legs and bosoms but they're covered, there are fights but there's no knives going in or slashed faces.

Now, when I see re-runs of the show, I'm proud of it. Sometimes I'm surprised by scenes I'd forgotten or I'll think: 'Cor, that was funny.' Even though I've

long since lost the ability to walk through walls, this book has brought back many wonderful memories of *Randall & Hopkirk (deceased)* – and it's nice to know that this time, thanks to the power of the printed word, there is more than one person out there who can hear what I'm saying!

Chapter One
When the Spirit Moves You
The Origins of
Randall & Hopkirk (deceased)

Never was there a better time to be a damsel in distress than in the 1960s and early 1970s. No need to learn self-defence, carry a personal alarm or a photograph of Germaine Greer, all a girl had to do was look winsome and helpless and before she could say 'Danger Man', a chivalrous male hero would arrive to rescue her. They came along more frequently than buses – *The Saint, Adam Adamant, The Baron, The Persuaders, The Protectors, The Adventurer* and many more. They all combined to ensure that no matter what atrocities were being committed in the real world, as far as television was concerned, the crime clear-up rate was 100 per cent.

Many of these shows emanated from ITC, the overseas arm of Lew Grade's ATV, and it was there that the two guiding lights of *Randall & Hopkirk*

(deceased), creator Dennis Spooner and producer Monty Berman, first met.

Londoner Monty Berman started out in the film industry as a camera assistant. During the War, he met up with fellow technician Robert S. Baker and together they went into partnership, producing a series of low-budget movies, the first being *Date With a Dream* which starred Norman Wisdom and Terry-Thomas. Baker and Berman then hit upon the idea of making true crime thrillers and enjoyed considerable success with adaptations of the Jack the Ripper murders and the escapades of body-snatchers Burke and Hare. This enabled them to move on to larger budget pictures, including three works from 1958 – the science fiction movie *The Trollenberg Terror; Blood of the Vampire,* a horror film starring Donald Wolfit;

A pyjama-clad Jeff Randall en route for his early-morning graveyard rendezvous with Marty.

Singer Happy Lee and a beatnik (Ronald Lacey) help Jeff and the police with their enquiries in 'My Late, Lamented Friend and Partner'.

and the acclaimed war epic *Sea of Sand*, featuring a distinguished cast headed by Richard Attenborough.

But the real turning point for Baker and Berman came when they acquired the television rights to Leslie Charteris's character, The Saint. With Roger Moore beneath the halo of Simon Templar, the series was a worldwide success, being sold to some 80 countries and accumulating sales of over £370 million. Then followed *Gideon's Way,* a noble police tale starring John Gregson (a stalwart from *Sea of Sand*), before the pair went their separate ways.

Berman's took him to another ITC series, *The Baron,* where in 1965 he met up with established scriptwriter Dennis Spooner. It was to prove a fruitful relationship for both parties. Spooner later recalled: 'I had written shows with Terry Nation; Monty Berman was producing shows with Bob Baker. But because they'd got it to a fine art between them on *The Saint,* it really got to the point where you just didn't need two producers of their capability and standing working on a television show. I mean, they'd made major movies, and here they were, two producers, turning out a show and their talents weren't extended in any way. So somebody – I presume it was Lew Grade – said: "Look, this is ridiculous, the two of you on one show. Let's split you up and you can do a show each – then we'll get twice as much product and you've each got your own show."'

So when *Gideon's Way* ended, Baker continued with *The Saint* while Berman moved on to produce *The Baron.* Terry Nation, best known for creating Dr.

Who's arch enemies the Daleks, served as script editor on *The Baron,* a role which apparently he did not greatly enjoy. Either alone or in conjunction

Jeff tries to force a confession out of the beatnik, knowing that he witnessed Marty's murder.

with Nation, Spooner wrote almost half of the 30 adaptations of John Creasey's novels which starred Steve Forrest as John Mannering, an American antiques dealer based in London. *The Baron* was well received and Berman and Spooner became firm friends. Through Berman's own production company, Filmakers (later rechristened Scoton), the two began to discuss ideas for future projects. Spooner was particularly keen on a series based around The Incredible Wilson, a character he had remembered from reading *Wizard* magazine as a boy. The rights to the character, a boys' own hero boasting enormous strength and supposedly winning every

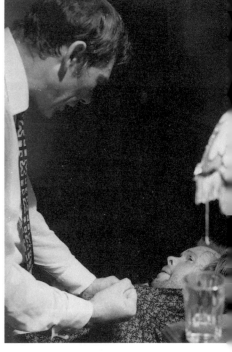

Olympic event single-handed, were not actually available but Spooner was undeterred. Peeling away at a slight tangent, he came up with the notion of three secret agents with special powers. They were called *The Champions.*

Randall & Hopkirk (deceased) | **11**

1. When the Spirit Moves You

This first collaboration between Berman and Spooner (the latter also acted as script supervisor, Terry Nation having returned to writing scripts instead of editing them) proved so popular that Lew Grade and ITC eagerly financed further series. In March 1968, Berman and Spooner thought up *Department S,* which was to star Peter Wyngarde as flamboyant investigator Jason King. It was a highly individual series but nothing compared to Dennis Spooner's next brainchild.

Spooner had long been interested in the paranormal and, inspired by several feature films (including Hal Roach's *Topper* series, *Here Comes Mr. Jordan* and Noel Coward's *Blithe Spirit*), he contemplated the possibility of a television series featuring a ghost as a regular character. It was decided that a detective show would offer the greatest scope for storylines and so Spooner prepared the ground for *Randall & Hopkirk (deceased),* a detective duo in which one partner was a ghost.

Monty Berman recalls: 'Dennis and I worked in adjoining offices at the Elstree Studios. One day, he said he had an idea for a series which was rather unusual and when he told me about it, I had to agree with him! Whenever we were trying to sell a show, Dennis would write down something like a six-line outline and I would go and put the idea to Lew Grade in his office at 7 am, and Lew would say yes or no – just like that. Because films had been made along similar themes, I was confident that *Randall & Hopkirk* would work. I thought it was a jolly good idea – a good twist. And Lew said yes.'

But Lew Grade was not immediately smitten with the proposal, possibly because he thought that the lack of a leading American man would inhibit overseas sales or indeed that its cavalier treatment of death might offend. Fortunately for Berman and Spooner, the synopsis caught the eye of Australian Ralph Smart, who had served as producer, writer and director on such series as *The Adventures of Robin Hood, The Invisible Man* and *Danger Man.* Smart was impressed. Dennis Spooner remembered: 'Ralph Smart was a sort of father figure as a far as ATV goes. He saw the concept and thought it was terrific. He said: "I wanna write the pilot!" I was delighted that he wrote the pilot because that convinced Lew that we should make the series.'

Spooner's more detailed outline described just two principal characters; firstly Steven Randall. 'Ambitious. In his late twenties, early thirties. A direct, blunt, honest man of tall, athletic build. Handsome. A man of action who prefers to settle an argument with his fists rather than with a persuasive logic. Women approve of him – to say the least. Headstrong, but just and fair. Once he takes a case he sees it through to the end, even if it begins to look as though it may break him, or lose him his licence. He shows a respect for the law, but he will go his own way if he has to. He never sits on the fence. Steve Randall always takes sides.'

Martin Hopkirk: 'of around the same age as his partner but physically very different. Chubby. A friendly man. Likeable. A humorous character. Kind. Accident prone – things never quite work out as planned, but, there's always the next time.'

Spooner continued: 'Randall and Hopkirk operate a private investigation agency with a head office (their only office) situated in the West End of London. They boast a fashionable, yet cheap, address.

'They have been in business for several years. The rewards have been adequate, rather than spectacular. The general humdrum routine of lost dogs, missing persons, and the tailing of husbands for suspicious wives, has occasionally been shattered by the "big break"...but this type of peak has been very rare.

Marty is always on hand to lend advice – whether it's wanted or not.

Filming the fight scene from 'The Smile Behind the Veil'.

'Steve Randall however, is ambitious. An optimist, he is quite convinced that given the break, he can do more than make a go of it – he can get to the top. Large retainers for security firms, insurance companies, and huge private concerns are there for the taking. A few spectacular successes and the firm of Randall & Hopkirk will definitely be going places.

'Marty Hopkirk is not so convinced – but so what? As far as he is concerned, things are not too bad as they are – they make a living, work for themselves, and have a good time. And how many people can boast as much as that?

'This is the basic situation as our series begins. No, there's nothing very dramatic about it. In fact a comparatively normal, usual situation, with two likeable, uncomplicated people.

'BUT...the firm of Randall & Hopkirk are working on one of those very rare, large, and important cases, and the circumstances we find them in prove tragic. MARTY HOPKIRK IS KILLED.

'Steve Randall is shattered. No, Hopkirk was not the greatest thing since Sherlock Holmes. As a matter of fact he was always accident-prone anyway, but he was a partner, a friend, loyal. And Steve Randall takes the death very badly, he blames himself personally that it happened at all, and is all for winding up the business.

'Marty Hopkirk, of course, knows the true facts. His death was entirely his own fault. More to the point he ruined any success the company might have had, and it could take years for the business to get over it. Marty Hopkirk's ghost does not go to

1. When the Spirit Moves You

14

In 'Money to Burn', Jeff's only companion in custody is Marty. Still, at least he ate his greens.

wherever it is all respecting, departing spirits go. He will stay on Earth and make amends!'

Spooner then went on to discuss the effect of Marty's decision to hang around.

'Now what happens when a ghost decides to remain in the crime-breaking business, as a detective? And with a partner who is still living and unaware of him!

'True, in Hopkirk's position, working on a case, he is able to do many things. To walk through walls for example, and listen in to any conversation completely unobserved, between even the criminals themselves. But armed with the knowledge of their plan – then what?

'You see, unfortunately for Hopkirk, ghosts find contact with living persons very difficult. I mean, few people can actually talk to a ghost.

'However, Hopkirk is determined. The company of Randall & Hopkirk is to be put on a sound footing

come what may. He will find a way – even if it is a ghostly one. And that, come to think of it, is the only sort available.

'There are disadvantages too in being a ghost. Slipping through walls may be useful but this sort of thing backfires. I mean, if you jump into a suspect's car to eavesdrop, and it pulls away you are left sitting in the road! Although to balance this, a poltergeist, capable of heaving heavy cases, can be very useful in a fight.'

This then was Dennis Spooner's vision of *Randall & Hopkirk (deceased)* in early 1968 but a number of changes, major and minor, took place before the series hit the screen in September 1969. The most obvious was the amendment of Randall's first name to Jeff. He also lost most of his ambition together with a good deal of his attraction to women. For while there were the statutory pretty girls, an essential ingredient of most adventure series of the day (particularly those being sold to America), the vast majority found Jeff quite resistible, although in fairness, Marty's habit of materialising at the most inopportune moments did little to improve his partner's chances.

And talking of women, what of Jeannie? Spooner originally made no mention of Marty leaving behind a widow but the role was created to conform to ITC's practice of including a female lead in their sixties series – witness Cordelia Winfield in *The Baron*, Sharron Macready in *The Champions* and Annabelle Hurst from *Department S.*

Marty himself was transformed from being accident-prone into a born worrier but the biggest alteration to his lifestyle was his ability to communicate. Dennis Spooner had stated that Randall could never see or hear his ghostly partner but it was soon realised that this state of affairs would be too restrictive, denying any real interplay between the two prinicpals. Thus in the first episode, 'My Late, Lamented Friend And Partner', the ghost of Marty announces in the misty cemetery that Jeff will be the only person able to see and hear him.

'You're the only one, Jeff...I chose you. Apart from the odd manifestation, nobody'll see me...I choose you, Jeff.'

Prior to this production decision, Spooner had outlined three instances as to how Marty would be able to communicate with the other side. All three were later incorporated in episodes. One was via jumping a queue of waiting spirits at a meeting of the British Spiritualist Society (this scene was to appear in 'The Trouble With Women'); another was through an upturned wine glass at a seance party ('Who Killed Cock Robin?'); and the third utilised an elderly psychic lady who could see and hear Marty but, just when it looked as though she would serve as a permanent contact, she too died. The little old lady became Mrs. Pleasance in 'For The Girl Who Has Everything'.

By the time *Randall & Hopkirk (deceased)* went into production in the summer of 1968, the characterisations had been finalised.

Jeff Randall

The alive half of the partnership. A down-at-heel gumshoe still struggling to pay the rent after years in the business, principally because of a tendency to accept cases with little financial reward. That he does so is due to the fact that, beneath his grizzled exterior, lies a sympathetic soul, always ready to help out what he considers to be a deserving cause. On other occasions, he accepts dubious assignments purely for the money even though his brain – and Marty – warn

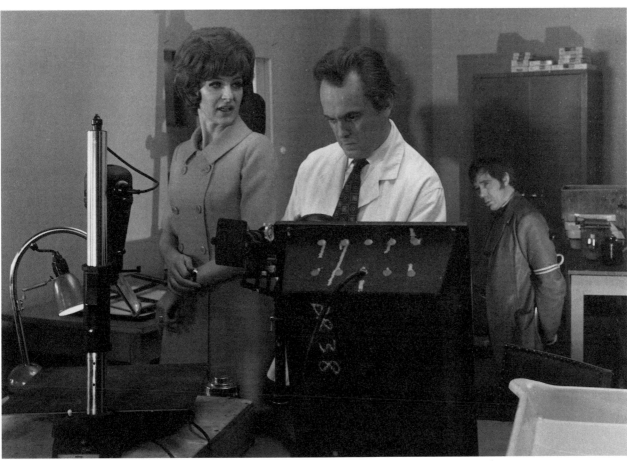

Jeff looks on helplessly while Karen Howarth (Caroline Blakiston) and her henchman Rawlins (Philip Madoc) make final adjustments to a micro-camera in 'Never Trust a Ghost'.

him of the consequences. Although handy with his fists, Jeff has an unfortunate habit of being beaten to a pulp every episode. He nevertheless boasts a certain rugged charm and it would not be improbable for him to be seen with a girl on each arm. Sadly, it often looks as though one has also recently sat on his face. But Jeff is something of a reluctant romeo, possibly because most of the women with whom he becomes involved in the line of duty are responsible for his being rendered unconscious, locked in a darkened cellar, thrown in a police cell or ending up at the foot of a well. That sort of thing can put a chap off women. He is particularly careful where Jean Hopkirk is concerned, being fearful of incurring the jealous wrath of the attendant Marty. Jeff also manages to land himself in frequent bother with the police. Since he seems to be either present at, or knows of, every murder or robbery that has been committed, Jeff is always one step ahead of the police – admittedly not a difficult task for a force which gives the impression that it is still conducting house-to-house enquiries in the hunt for Crippen. And how can he explain to the boys in blue that the reason he knows so much is because his informant is a ghost? No wonder they think he needs locking up!

Marty Hopkirk

Killed off while working on an apparently routine divorce case, Marty returns as a ghost to solve the riddle of his murder and recreate the partnership with Jeff. Dressed all in white (the original Dennis Spooner specification was for pale green), the ghostly Marty turns out to be just as big a worrier when dead as he was when he was alive. He worries about the business, the car, Jeff's driving, everybody else's driving, but, above all, he worries about his widow Jeannie. Marty cannot bear the thought of her being seen with another man. If he had perfected the trick, he would have been beside himself when Emil Cavallo-Smith took a shine to Jean in the episode 'Vendetta For A Dead Man'. Via Jeff, of course, Marty tells Jean that she should stop seeing Emil.

'Who says so?' she asks.

'I do,' replies Jeff hesitantly.

At that, Jean sidles over to him and says: 'Why Jeff...why, that's the nicest thing you've said to me for a long time.'

'What does that mean?' demands Marty, whereupon Jeff retreats to a safe distance from Jean's amorous advances.

And when he catches Jeff and Jeannie together in their night-clothes in a scene from 'Never Trust A Ghost' (she is actually providing Jeff with nothing more than an alibi), Marty angrily insists that the police arrest his partner. Only once perceived as a lonely figure, when walking the streets in 'Never Trust A Ghost', Marty is generally, despite his angst, a likeable, quick-witted spectre. It is he who repeatedly rescues Jeff from life-or-death situations, usually by ingenious methods which suggest that, when living, he was a far better detective than his partner ever gave him credit for. Indeed, it would seem that Marty was the brains of the outfit and Jeff the brawn. As a ghost, Marty has the definite advantage of being uncatchable, except in 'Whoever Heard Of A Ghost Dying?' where a clairvoyant attempts to exorcise him. Marty's

Another fine mess... Jeff inspects the damage in 'Whoever Heard of a Ghost Dying?'

party piece is walking through walls although he can also produce a very nice hurricane and, with extreme concentration, can shatter mirrors. He has also been known to make cups vibrate (in 'But What A Sweet Little Room') and, in 'Never Trust A Ghost', to jolt a typewriter into action. But perhaps his most irritating trick is his ability to vanish into thin air (to the sound of a harpsichord) when losing an argument with Jeff, thereby leaving his opponent talking to himself. Think how useful that could be on *Question Time...*

Jean Hopkirk

Marty's attractive blonde widow cuts a somewhat melancholy figure as she grieves for her lost spouse. To keep the business going, she acts as Jeff's secretary, a role which inevitably drags her far beyond the realms of filing cabinets into situations which place her own life in jeopardy. Fortunately, the unseen Marty is always on hand to bail her out and to

make sure that her friendship with Jeff remains exactly that. She continues to live in the same flat, number 8, (it mysteriously became 21 in 'Could You Recognise The Man Again?') as when Marty was alive and assumes the ownership of Marty's red Mini. When Jeff borrows it for 'A Disturbing Case' and 'You Can Always Find A Fall Guy', he is subjected to a stream of abuse from Marty about excessive speed and jumpy gear changes. Being unaware that her late husband can communicate from beyond the grave, Jean is naturally puzzled to find Jeff apparently talking to himself in 'A Disturbing Case'. So she and her sister Jennifer have poor Randall carted off to a clinic for treatment.

Marty takes a dim view as Jeff's hand settles on Jeannie's shoulder.

Jeff and Jeannie attempt to fend off the mechanical mayhem caused by the Foster brothers in 'All Work and No Pay'.

Either as a cost-cutting exercise or an attempt to speed up filming, *Randall & Hopkirk (deceased)* was filmed side-by-side with *Department S*. Monty Berman produced *Randall & Hopkirk*, with Dennis Spooner given the grandiose title of executive story consultant.

Cyril Frankel was appointed creative consultant, a role which had him responsibility for the show's style and overall look. In addition, Frankel directed six episodes, including the all-important pilot, 'My Late, Lamented Friend And Partner'.

Monty Berman says: 'I used directors with whom I had worked before. Cyril had worked with me on Gideon's Way, *The Baron* and *The Champions* while Roy Ward Baker, Ray Austin, Paul Dickson, Leslie Norman, Jeremy Summers and Robert Tronson had all worked on one or more of my other series. It was the same with all of the crew. We had worked together on a number of shows and they were very experienced technicians. Being an ex-technician myself, we all spoke the same language so I was able to convey exactly what was needed.'

Similarly, Dennis Spooner had his pool of tried and tested writers. Between them, Tony Williamson and Donald James accounted for 20 of the 26 episodes of *Randall & Hopkirk*. 'I had known Tony Williamson since we had done army service together,' said Spooner. 'He worked in this dental surgery at an army camp where the dentist was an absolute lunatic. I had a toothache and decided there was no way I was going to see him. So Tony and I broke into the surgery late one night and he pulled my tooth out! Donald James just walked into the office one day with *The Champions'* story "The Invisible Man", where the man has something implanted in his ear. I liked it so much that he became a regular part of the team.'

Two of the episodes were written by Gerald Kelsey who, among other things, penned *Dixon of Dock Green* for 14 years. 'I knew Dennis after he had approached me to do scripts first for *Dr. Who* and then *The Prisoner*. He liked my *Prisoner* script and so he asked me to work on his series. One day, he called me in to Elstree and showed me the script for "My Late, Lamented Friend And Partner". That pilot episode was his guideline. I took it away, studied it and wrote something in a similar vein. In fact, I used something very much like the car accident which Ralph Smart wrote in "My Late, Lamented Friend And Partner" for an episode of *Department S*. I enjoyed writing for *Randall & Hopkirk* and if I hadn't been so busy with *Dixon,* I would probably have written more than just the two episodes.'

With the series earmarked for the United States (it was syndicated there under the title *My Partner The Ghost* in 1972), a number of factors had to be borne in mind. 'With shows for the U.S., there were always certain things you had to watch,' says Monty Berman. 'You had to be careful that any humour translated and that the actors' accents were not too strong. In *Randall & Hopkirk*, the language of comedy was universal – it was more situation than dialogue. And we never considered having an American lead. Lew probably thought the series was so different that he could sell it without one.'

First to be cast was Mike Pratt although rumour has it that Irish comic Dave Allen had previously been considered for the role of Jeff! Pratt was another ITC regular, having appeared in episodes of *Danger Man, The Saint, Gideon's Way, The Baron* and *The Champions.* 'We thought Mike would be ideal for the role,' adds Berman. 'He had just the touch we needed for the character of Randall.'

Casting Marty proved tougher. 'We had Mike Pratt,' says Cyril Frankel, 'but we didn't know who to put with him. We had considered a few people but that's as far as it ever got. At that time in London, Italian restaurants were just starting out and I patronised Trattoria Paratza in Soho. I was there one

evening and at the next table was Kenneth Cope with his wife. Suddenly it occurred to me that he was right, so I went to see Monty the next day and said: "I saw someone last night who's right for the part of the ghost." We gave him a screen test, which I directed, and he got the part.'

Kenneth Cope remembers: 'I had to audition for the part of Marty although they told me afterwards that they had already made their minds up. I went to Elstree where they had built the cemetery and I had to do the scene where Marty is forced back to the grave and I say: "Only you can see me, Jeff! Only you!" I hadn't worked with Mike until then yet he took the time and trouble to come and tell me a couple

of days later that I'd got the part. He came to my house and we went out for dinner that night, and he told me that I had already been cast and that ITC had just wanted to make sure. He was a good lad, Michael.'

Australian actress Annette André was the obvious choice to play Jean after losing out to Alexandra Bastedo for the role of Sharron Macready in *The Champions* on the whim of an executive from the American CBS network. She was well known to the production team, having appeared in six episodes of *The Saint* as well as *The Baron*.

So the three principals were cast. All that remained now was to adhere to Dennis Spooner's principles.

He's behind you.

Chapter Two
The Smile Behind the Veil
Behind the Scenes on the Series

The early episodes in production remained faithful to Dennis Spooner's desire for a quirky, off-beat thriller. There was an abundance of fake spiritualists, eccentric mediums, ghost hunters and haunted houses in episodes such as 'But What A Sweet Little Room' and 'For The Girl Who Has Everything'. Kenneth Cope particularly enjoyed the involvement of other ghosts or people who, for one reason or another, could see Marty. It provided him with another performer to act and react to besides Mike Pratt. But after a while, word got back that the Americans were worried about this flippant treatment of death, and so the stories began to adopt a more straightforward detective format. It was this change of direction which caused considerable friction behind the scenes.

Kenneth Cope states: '75 per cent of the comedy in *Randall & Hopkirk* came from Mike and I. We battled like crazy to get comedy in. I had fierce argu-

Preparation for a scene from 'You Can Always Find a Fall Guy'.

With more than a little help from Marty, Jeff performs his mind-reading act to the audience for 'That's How Murder Snowballs'.

ments with Monty Berman about it. The show was aimed at the American market, or rather the mid-Atlantic, and they were worried about being able to understand English actors and all that rubbish, and they didn't want comedy or humour. But I think that's the thing that made the series the success it was.

'Take the episode "That's How Murder Snowballs" which features a music hall. The original scene had Michael standing in the wings, and I appear next to him. I said to the director, Ray Austin: "Let's have a bit of fun," as I was desperate to get comedy into it. "Let me appear at the wrong side by accident, as it's always funny when the ghost appears in the wrong place. Let me be shy at first walking across the stage with the chorus girls, then let me do a dance and let me get confident, go back, do it again and then come along and play the rest of the scene." And at the end of that little sequence, Jeff says to me: "You're a frustrated hoofer." That made

2. The Smile Behind the Veil

people laugh, yet all of that business was put in by me. Luckily, Ray Austin had a sense of humour.

'For the episode "Somebody Just Walked Over My Grave", there was a scene where Marty wanted to get away to watch England play football. My idea for a bit of business was that we should get some old footage of England playing in white and Bobby Charlton just coming back from scoring a goal. I said, you should see me blowing the ball into the net and then superimpose me running about with Bobby, celebrating – I'd just helped Bobby score a goal for England. And I'd get back to Jeff and say: "What do you think of that? I've always wanted to do that." It was so simple and would have been good for a laugh but they said: "No, it would cost too much money." So instead they built a little stand in the studio with a dozen extras cheering, and that was it.'

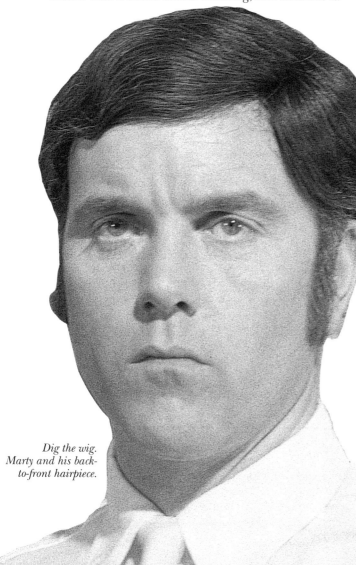

Dig the wig. Marty and his back-to-front hairpiece.

Cyril Frankel concedes: 'I started off with certain intentions which became somewhat lost as the series progressed. When I wasn't directing an episode, Kenneth Cope was apt to make his scenes more comic and that led to a little friction between us. My idea for *Randall & Hopkirk* was to make the series fairly realistic with this afterlife fantasy element, and the comedy was supposed to come from the ghost, while Monty wanted a private detective side of things as serious as Humphrey Bogart. I think I got all that in the pilot.

'It was a different style of comedy. Ken would say: "Cyril, you're stopping it being funny!", and I'd reply that it must be realistic and have a balance between the serious and the comedy as I wanted people laughing with us not at us. He could get away with what he wanted with other directors but not with me. However, despite this slight difference of opinion, he was a nice man but whether he was right or I was right, I don't know.'

In a 1986 interview with *Time Screen* magazine, Dennis Spooner said: 'There were different theories from the people buying the series as to how it should work. To a certain extent I was under pressure in so far as if we did one that was very funny, and some of them were very, very funny, people would get a bit scared and think: "God, this is almost a comedy, and really we're supposed to be making a detective series." So it hovered about a bit.'

Meanwhile Kenneth Cope had other things on his mind or, to be more precise, his head. He had not worn a wig for the screen test but it was decided that he should for the series. 'Unfortunately,' he

says, 'I had it on back to front for at least the first two episodes, maybe even the third. We had this Canadian hairdresser and she didn't know which way it had to go. Neither did I. It was all right but I looked like the middle one of The Three Stooges!

'Nobody noticed, nobody said anything until I said to the hairdresser: "Shouldn't it be the other way round?"

'So she tried it that way. I said: "This looks much better – you can see more of my eyes!" To be honest, it never bothered me that much – not like one bald actor I remember who always wore a wig. And if the part called for him to be bald, rather than take the wig off, he'd wear a bald wig on top of his own one!'

Apart from the wig, Marty's other famous appendage was his white suit. 'I had five in all,' says Kenneth Cope, 'all made of silk and bought from Saville Row. They were very expensive. They had no pockets but creases could be a problem and make-up used to get on to them sometimes – I don't know how because we were all so very careful. But if there was a mark, it would be covered up with white stuff, a bit like Tipp-Ex, until it was dry-cleaned again.

'The suits had to be ironed, pressed and dry-cleaned every time I used them. We had strange actresses coming in for an episode, and I'd rehearse it with jeans, a white shirt and a white tie on. Then I'd put the rest of the gear on, on the set because there would be no time to be modest and go to a separate changing room, and as soon as the director said: "That's a print", my jacket and trousers used to come

off. So there was I, a leading man, stripping off in front of a perfect stranger! I was left with my white boots and shirt and I'd put my jeans back on. It was simply that everyone was so worried about coffee getting spilt on the suit.

'The white boots were all very well but whenever I put my feet up on a desk, you could see the black soles. We started off by putting felt, a bit like the green baize of a billiard table, on the soles of the shoes so that when I walked about, there wouldn't be a noise. But after a while people seemed to accept the fact that I was walking about and wearing footwear. They were accepting the character as a ghost, rather than criticising and saying, "How can he do that?"

'In a way,' continues Cope, 'mine was the easiest part of the three because I could look at the others, whereas Mike Pratt was the only other one who could look at me. But what I had to remember all the time was that I dared not touch anything. As a ghost, I would go right through it. It's a natural thing, for instance, to lean up against a mantelpiece. But only a human can do this. I suppose the hardest thing was knowing what to do with my hands.'

The major difficulty facing Kenneth Cope's fellow actors, apart from Mike Pratt, was remembering that although he was actually in scenes, they were supposed to be unaware of his presence. 'That was more difficult than you might imagine,' recalls Annette André, 'because it's not easy to keep your eyes off someone who is with you. You can't control normal reactions. We had one scene, for instance,

2. The Smile Behind the Veil

Timothy West as Sam Grimes attackes Jeff with a chair in 'Vendetta for a Dead Man'.

when Ken Cope was supposed to walk past me, but very close to me, without my knowing he was there. As it happened, my hand was a little way in front of me and I instinctively pulled it back so that he wouldn't touch it as he went past. Jean, of course, wouldn't have done that.'

The scripts on *Randall & Hopkirk (deceased)* relied heavily on special effects and it was thanks to the technical expertise of the assembled crew that Marty was able to walk through walls and materialise or disappear at a moment's notice. The technique for the latter is known as 'jump cutting'.

'It was fairly straightforward,' says Kenneth Cope. 'I closed my eyes to tip everybody off and they would have to freeze and then I would exit the scene. Then they'd say, "Action" and they'd continue, and my movement would be cut out. As I say, it was quite easy to do – you just cut the tape and you've lost me.'

'For entering a scene, it was all done in reverse. At a rehearsed point, the director would shout, "Freeze" and everyone would stand dead still, exactly

as they were, while the art director waited for things like the cigarette smoke to settle down. Then they'd call me, I'd walk to my mark and the director would shout, "Action". Then Jeff would react to me if he had to. As for the others, they had time not to blink because they could see me standing there and there was a bit of a pause before action resumed. I was supposed to get in as quick as I could but after a while I just used to saunter in – that was me being wicked!'

Walking through walls was achieved by use of an old theatre trick called 'Pepper's Ghost'. 'It was a difficult exercise,' says Cope, 'and was costly because it took such a long time to set up. What they did was put a plain piece of glass at an angle in front of the camera lens. Meanwhile, I was behind the camera against a big piece of black velvet cloth hanging from the gantry. When they wanted to see me, they'd put a light on me and the image would be reflected on the plain glass. The camera was photographing the mirror image of me behind it. So if I had to go right in the script, I had to go left in reality. The time-consuming element was trying to get the reflection to match up with what was happening on the set and getting the sizes right, because I would be something like 40 feet away. I was completely on my own. If I was playing a scene with Jeff, talking to him and walking through a wall, I was a long way away. It was quite a lonely job sometimes.'

What of Marty's other tricks? 'I was always into card games,' remembers Cope. 'I could cheat, as in the episode "The Trouble With Women". I could go and watch women undressing if I'd wanted to with my powers, but we kept right away from that except in "A Sentimental Journey" where Marty is forced to retrieve a note from a woman in a shower. The only time I got naughty was in "Just For The Record" when I put my arm around Miss Russia when she was sitting next to me on a settee, but then my wife came in. But that was another bit of business that had been put in, the ghost being a little naughty and then being caught out. Mike and I used to work together and suggest things – the blowing, the disappearing and the walking through walls were all well-known technical effects, and they were all written into the scripts. Now and again, someone would come up with ideas and they did them, but the idea had to be simple and had to work quickly, otherwise the whole production would be held up. We did a lot of blowing in the first few episodes which was a bit dodgy as they had to have a wind machine. I joked with Leslie Norman, who directed one of those early episodes: "Go easy on the wind machine, it's blowing my wig off!"

The weird and wonderful Foster brothers (Dudley Foster and Alfred Burke) bid farewell at the end of 'All Work and No Pay'.

2. The Smile Behind the Veil

'It took a total of 14 months to make the 26 shows. The episodes were shot on a two-week turn-around but we missed shots and had to pick them up when we could, often on Sundays. We'd miss bits from one episode and have to roll over to the next director's episode. So we didn't really have any rest.'

Such a hectic schedule inevitably took its toll. Annette André was taken ill and had to miss two episodes so it was thought prudent to invent a sister, Jennifer (played by Judith Arthy), who conveniently acted as Jeff's secretary in 'The House On Haunted Hill' while Jean was 'away'. 'I didn't like missing those episode at all,' says Annette, 'but I really was laid low.'

But that was nothing to the chaos which resulted from the celebrations for Mike Pratt's 38th birthday. Kenneth Cope recalls: 'We had finished shooting for the day and went off to Michael's dressing-room for some champagne. Having been told we could go, we made the fatal error of not leaving the building because a little while later they pulled us back to do a shot in a car in front of a backdrop of a city skyline. The backdrop was on a big drum which was then revolved to make it look as if the car was moving. In fact, the car was perfectly still. They dressed us and we weren't falling-about-drunk, just happy. We came

to do this scene and I got in to the car at what was supposed to be 90 mph. We heard somebody say: "Action....Action....Action."

'Mike said to me: "It's you, isn't it?"

'I said: "No, it's you."

'Somehow we managed to do it but it was hysterical. Mike's arms were supposed to be frozen to the wheel but they were anyway – it had nothing to do with the script.

'After that, Mike carried on with the party and went back to his flat in Eaton Place. One of his stand-ins was with him. Mike had lost his keys and was locked out. The stand-in climbed a drainpipe, up two or three floors, got in, came down and opened the front door. It was solved. Michael, being Michael, said: "I can do that." But as he shinned up the pipe, he fell 20 feet into the basement area and broke both his legs.'

With Mike Pratt unable to walk, this caused a major crisis since filming was just about to begin on the final episode of the series, a story written by Gerald Kelsey entitled 'The Dead Don't Even Whisper'.

Kelsey remembers: 'One morning, Dennis Spooner called me and said we had a terrible problem. He said that the night before Mike Pratt had been trying to copy his exploits in the studio and had broken both his legs. The thing was we had 25 episodes in the can but had to have another one. You can't sell 25 – you can only sell 13 or 26. Lew was facing disaster. The entire second half of the series would have been wasted as far as overseas sales were concerned.

'So Dennis said: "We must have another one. Can you rewrite the story as if it were episode one, prior to Marty being killed? Can you redo it with Jeff in a hospital bed?"

'What I did was virtually reverse the parts. Instead of Marty being incapacitated as a ghost, it was Jeff who was incapacitated in bed with his legs in plaster, having fallen from a balcony. I practically

'The Ghost Talks' – the aftermath of Mike Pratt's birthday.

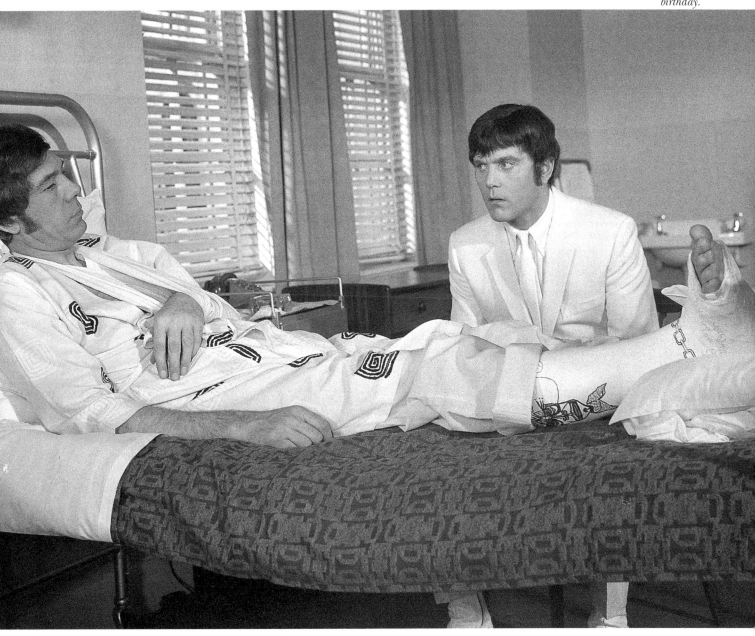

gave Jeff's lines to Marty and vice-versa and so it was Marty who ended up in the sauna instead of Jeff. I rewrote it all in about three days and the episode went out as "The Ghost Talks."'

Thus while Mike Pratt lay in a genuine hospital bed in the studio, with a nurse in daily attendance, Kenneth Cope as Marty did all the running about. 'I took over the script that Mike was supposed to do,'

says Cope. 'That's how we got round it. It was done as a reprise. There was all that "I was a better detective than you" stuff and we would keep going back to the bed where I was telling Mike what was going on.

'It was nice playing a live guy at the very end. I was able to open doors and walk through them instead of having to glide through them, and I could drive cars and talk to people. It made a pleasant

2. The Smile Behind the Veil

change because it was very difficult keeping up the believability that when I'm in the room with another person who can't see me, I try to talk to them. For instance, when I'm with that football commentator in "Somebody Just Walked Over My Grave" and saying "Give me the score", why have I suddenly forgotten that he can't hear me? It was difficult to do, and I had to work at it to make it believable. But the best thing about that final episode was that I was allowed to smoke. They were very good to me. Michael had a cigarette allowance and even though I was a ghost and couldn't smoke, I was given an allowance as well!

'I also had three doubles and a stand-in. Mike had doubles and stand-ins too. He used to have a fist fight with his stand-in every Friday night just to keep in trim. The stand-ins were used mainly for long shots. I remember Mike and I got angry because our stand-ins were getting fat. There would be shots of them getting out of a car in the distance, walking towards the camera, and they were waddling! We made them go on a diet.'

One of the regular stunt men on *Randall & Hopkirk* was Alf Joint, currently Stunt Co-Ordinator

on *London's Burning* and who in the past has doubled for such diverse personalities as Marlon Brando on the film *Superman* and Lee Remick in *The Omen*! He says: 'Most of the stunts on *Randall & Hopkirk* were fairly routine – falling over balconies, staircases and so on. Frank Maher was the actual stunt arranger. I remember on the show we had an Irish stunt guy, who's now dead, and who liked a drink or two. And while Mike Pratt was away, this Irish chap was given Mike's dressing-room. Now Mike was also fond of a drink and the stunt man found a bottle of vodka in Mike's fridge. Unfortunately, it went to this guy's head and he started throwing another stunt man, Bill Cummins, who was merely trying to pacify him, all around the studio bar. Everyone rushed up to see what the commotion was and in the end, five policemen arrived to cart the Irishman away. The irony was that at the time on *Randall & Hopkirk*, he was playing a policeman...'

Cyril Frankel recalls a different problem with a stunt man on *Randall & Hopkirk*. 'On "Vendetta For A Dead Man", I tried to do the episode in basically two colours – green and brown with various shades of beige. This covered both sets and costumes. Anyway, I had to shoot this chap coming over a wall, which was really just behind the studios, and I had an agreement with wardrobe that they would provide green overalls. This was the final day of shooting and I only had time for the one take. The stunt guy came over the wall and the overalls were blue! Afterwards I complained to wardrobe and she replied that it didn't matter. So my concept for this episode had been somewhat lost.'

The majority of the filming took place in Elstree and surrounding areas, a region of England which has been immortalised on everything from the *On The Buses* film to *EastEnders* and *Grange Hill*. The Edgwarebury Hotel doubled as Merston Manor in 'The House On Haunted Hill' and as the Howe residence in 'Who Killed Cock Robin?', Elstree Aerodrome played the fictitious Longton Airfield in 'A Sentimental Journey', while many of the theatre scenes for 'That's How Murder Snowballs' were filmed at the Palace Theatre, Watford. The bridge over Tykes Water Lake, as used in the episode 'The Smile Behind The Veil', was seen on a more regular basis when it formed part of the opening title sequence to the Linda Thorson season of *The Avengers*. 'A Sentimental Journey'

Judith Arthy (standing) as Jeannie's sister, Jennifer, in 'A Disturbing Case'.

Hopkirk's office (in reality a soft
furnishings outlet in Harrow)
later fulfilled the same function
for Charlie Endell in the 1971
series *Budgie* which starred
Adam Faith. As for Marty, he
was killed in Maida Vale, North-
West London, the speeding car
actually travelling no faster than
a couple of stage hands could
push it!

Kenneth Cope remembers:
'We spent a lot of time in graveyards, because of the nature of
the programme, and I used to
have time whilst they were
setting the cameras and the
lighting up to go and look at
the records, especially those
concerning the First World
War. It was so depressing. You'd
see three people from the same
family aged 19, 21 and 22, all
killed in the First World War. It
stops you in your tracks. It can
get to you and you start to worry about cables going
across the graves and paper cups being left everywhere. It seemed like sacrilege.'

also reveals an ITC in-house joke where among the
graffiti scrawled on the walls of the Glasgow tenement
block is the famous Simon Templar stick-man.
Beneath it is written the blasphemous suggestion:
'The Saint Is Bent.' The exterior door to *Randall &*

Considerable use was also made of stock footage,
including Westminster Hospital in 'You Can Always

Jeff briefly appears as a ghost while close to drowning in 'The Smile Behind the Veil'.
The angler makes sure he wasn't one that got away.

joke that, if you were filming a scene in a bedroom, he would step out of the wardrobe and say "hello" in the middle of the shot. But that's Roger for you.

'Mike was into music and was always playing his guitar. He was also into Indian stuff. He always had incense in his dressing-room and he put his bed halfway up the wall to create more space, which made it look like a brothel. But it smelt like a nice place. My dressing-room was entirely different. It was functional, it was somewhere to kip. Annette André was next door to me, so we could chat. Linda Thorson was the other side. She left me her kettle when she packed in *The Avengers*.'

Find A Fall Guy', a train speeding through the night in 'A Sentimental Journey' and an owl (nicknamed 'the ITC owl' as it had graced countless other ITC series) in 'For The Girl Who Has Everything'. And the warehouse fire in 'Just For The Record' was filmed three years before the start of *Randall & Hopkirk (deceased)*. It happened when fire broke out in a warehouse near to the Elstree Studios and Monty Berman decided to film it, just in case it might come in useful for stock footage.

The episode 'It's Supposed To Be Thicker Than Water' used the famous 'White Jaguar' stock footage in which the car careers uncontrollably over the edge of a cliff and is smashed to pieces on the rocks some 200 feet below. It was featured in two episodes of *The Baron* as well as many other shows, even *Spitting Image*. The writer of that particular episode of *Randall & Hopkirk*, Tony Williamson, remembered how 'writers fought tooth and nail to get that White Jaguar footage for their episode on every new series!'

There were three permanent sets for *Randall & Hopkirk (deceased)* – Jeff's flat, Jeannie's apartment and the Randall & Hopkirk office. Other studio sets at Elstree tended to be interchangeable. 'A hell of a lot was going on there at the same time,' says Kenneth Cope. 'There was *The Avengers, The Saint, The Champions* and *Department S* besides ourselves. A lot of mixing went on. We all used to meet at lunch time – in fact we used each other's sets. We had a lot of library sets, which we borrowed from *The Saint*. In fact, our writers would deliberately incorporate a library scene into an episode so that we wouldn't have to build a set. Similarly, we had a doctor's waiting room so The Saint would come and use ours. It was all very handy. But you had to beware of Roger Moore. He had a favourite

It was not only the sets which jumped around from series to series. Fashion spotters will have observed that it was not unknown for Jean Hopkirk to be seen wearing one of Sharron Macready's outfits from *The Champions*. Jeff's white Vauxhall Victor had a cameo role in *Department S* while Marty's red Mini had previously appeared in an episode of *The Saint* and was later to pop up in *The Persuaders*.

The haunting harpsichord theme music for *Randall & Hopkirk* was composed by Edwin Astley, stalwart of *The Saint, Danger Man, The Baron, The Champions* and *Department S* plus numerous films such as *To Paris With Love, The Mouse That Roared*, the 1961 production of *Phantom Of The Opera* and *Digby, The Biggest Dog In The World*. He is also the father-in-law of The Who's Pete Townshend. In total, Edwin Astley scored 188 pieces of music for the series. How did he go about composing the theme for *Randall & Hopkirk (deceased)*? 'It's a matter of using something so distinc-

Marty prepares to make himself scarce while O'Malley (Roy Desmond) and Elizabeth Saxon (Sue Lloyd) watch the crooks' plane land at the conclusion of 'Money to Burn'.

tive that if you have the television on in the next room, you'd know that programme had started. It has to be something distinctive in the orchestration or the tune and I suppose that's why I used the harpsichord, because in those days it was a very distinctive sound. There's no mistaking the harpsichord. And the idea of using the minor key was obviously because of the "death" part of it.'

For all the differences of opinion over which path the series should follow, producer Monty Berman has fond memories of *Randall & Hopkirk (deceased)*. 'I'm not at all surprised it is still so popular. It was a very good series and, even though I say it myself, well done. We had completed making the shows before the first one was even transmitted so we didn't know how it would go down. Twenty-six was a lot to do unseen but Dennis and I had great confidence in the show. Ken and Mike came over so well that we thought it had every chance. The two boys were absolutely superb, the way they sparred off one another. And I must not forget the rest of the cast, even people like Ivor Dean who became a semi-regular as Inspector Large. I had worked with Ivor on *The Saint* when he played a similar role as Chief Inspector Teal. We had a pool of actors with whom we tended to work regularly. They knew us and so they knew what they were letting themselves in for.

'My favourite episode is "Murder Ain't What It Used To Be!" I liked that very much. David Healy was excellent as the American gangster and the scenes between his ghost and Hopkirk were first rate.'

Kenneth Cope says he does not have a favourite episode as such although he does have a soft spot for 'A Disturbing Case', the episode which Mike Pratt co-wrote. (According to Dennis Spooner, Mike 'just put it on my desk...'.) Cope says: 'That had a wonderful sequence with the foreign psychiatrist and Mike sleepwalking in a trance with me using the psychiatrist's voice to give him orders: "Hit him Jeff, hit him!" It was so funny. David Bauer, the guy playing the psychiatrist, dubbed my voice. I was supposed to be copying him but in fact he dubbed me. So all that "Hit him with the right, hit with the left" stuff wasn't me. I said the lines, but he came along and redubbed it in his own voice.

'It was a shame that we had to make the entire show before it was screened because I'm sure that we would have been allowed to introduce more comedy had we had an audience reaction to work with. Let's face it, when people remember *Randall & Hopkirk*, they talk about the comedy. To my mind, that's what made the show.

'But we did all the shows and then just walked away from it. It was another three or four months before the public got to see it and by that time the entire team had disbanded and moved onto other projects. I think that's why there was never a second series. By the time the interest had grown with the second repeats, it was far too late to go back to it.

'I'd like to have seen some fantastic things in the show, such as showing what happened to me in limbo. I wanted to come back and say, I've just had drinks with such and such who's dead, and make out I was having a great time wherever I was. But they wouldn't let me stick those sort of things in. I think they were over careful about the subject of my death. I suppose it was a bit of a taboo topic.'

Sensitive subject or not, it did not prevent *Randall & Hopkirk* being a hit in 35 countries from Argentina to Australia, Ghana to Guatemala, Malaysia to Mexico. The mind boggles as to what the good folk of Puerto Rico must have made of Marty.

Back in Blighty, Kenneth Cope made sure that he finished the series in style. 'The final take on the very last episode was shot at Pinewood Studios near the big sea tank used in war films. In fact, I'd used it as a bomb disposal person parachuting into the Atlantic in the film *Juggernaut*. But as soon as they said the final take on *Randall & Hopkirk* was OK, I just jumped into the muddy water with my white suit on. It was so important that nothing happened to the suits that this was the ultimate act of irreverence. But I'd been so fed up looking after that suit. It was such a relief...'

Inspector Large (Ivor Dean) eyeballs Jeff in 'Money to Burn'.

RIP
Chapter One

Chapter Three
The Ghost Talks
Kenneth Cope

Kenneth Cope will probably go down in history as the only person who has ever wanted to kiss Ena Sharples. Most men would prefer mouth-to-mouth contact with Desert Orchid but it was Ken's bold attempt to snatch a snog with the hair-netted harridan of Coronation Street that led to a crop of leading roles in the sixties, including that of Marty Hopkirk.

'I had a reputation for playing teddy boys at the time,' he recalls, 'and it was as a baddie that I went into Coronation Street as Jed Stone. I was in just the one episode and was supposed to do over Dennis Tanner because we'd been in prison together. Anyway, Ena Sharples got me against a wall under the viaduct and launched into a page of dialogue, telling me off and warning me away. At the very end, as she got closer and closer to me, I pulled a funny face and ad libbed: "Give us a kiss." It got a hell of a laugh from the crew and on the strength of that, Jed stayed for about five years on and off – and as a funny character rather than a bully.'

Jeff wakes up with another sore head in 'Just for the Record'.

Born in Liverpool, the son of an engineer, young Ken first made people laugh as a Boy Scout. 'My best mate was Norman Rossington, who went on to star in *The Army Game,* and we were both in the Scouts. In fact, we're still patrol leaders although we don't wear the shorts anymore. We were a very poor troop in those days. We used to do concert parties and collect jam-jars to go on scouting trips. We weren't even much good at collecting jam-jars because there was a sharp left turn into the Hartley's factory gates and we always used to lose a few off the cart. For the concerts, Norman and I did these crazy sketches which, amazingly, proved quite popular.

'As a result, Norman was invited to take part in a youth production of *The Merchant of Venice* at the David Lewis Theatre in Liverpool. I wasn't around when he was asked – I was ill or something – but he wouldn't go without me because he was too shy. So we both went and carried spears or whatever. Twelve months later, we both did auditions for the Bristol

Old Vic Theatre School. He was accepted and I joined him the following year. To get a grant, I had to audition for the Liverpool arts people. We both got our grants and managed to escape from Liverpool.

'It was a big step. At the time, I had been working in the drawing office at the Automatic Telephone Company where my father worked. It was

he who had got me the job there. He was a lovely man, and in those days to get your son a good job was all you could ask for.'

If Kenneth had any preconceptions about acting being a glamorous life, they were soon shattered. 'We had so little money, we used to live on chips and single cigarettes. I joined at Bristol as an assistant

'Vendetta for a Dead Man'. Marty saves Jeannie by using his powers to smash a mirror.

3. The Ghost Talks

All ghosts together: Bugsy Spanio (David Healy) and Marty in 'Murder Ain't What it Used to Be'.

theatre, and it was a sign of good luck if she made her presence felt. I don't really know whether I believe in ghosts or not. But it makes you think.

'After Bristol, Norman and I went off to do repertory in Cromer. We did two plays a week throughout a very hot summer. None of us got sunburnt because we were too busy learning our lines. We were so hard up that we used to rob the fridge of the digs we were in. The fridge had a chain on it to deter us and Norman was caught one night with his hand inside. The guy suddenly came down and Norman blurted out: "I thought I heard a rat."'

When Ken moved to London, he landed a job as a garage attendant in Hampstead. 'It was an ideal job for an aspiring young actor. It was only part-time but paid enough, with wages and tips, to ensure I ate regularly. But what was most important about that garage was that it was used by film and TV directors. So while checking their oil and wiping their windscreens, I used to chat to them and get tips about films scheduled for shooting and jobs in radio and TV.

'Basically, I lied and cheated my way into television. I told the directors that I'd done loads of telly in Canada – I'd never been to Canada in my life – and they used to say: "Yes, I think I've seen some of it."

'One of my first TV roles was in an episode of *The Adventures of Robin Hood* called "An Apple For The Archer". I played Timothy Cox, the man who introduced the Cox's Orange Pippin to England. I remember Paul Eddington was in it too as Pierre of Bordeaux – he also played Will Scarlett in other episodes. Anyway, Paul and I had to compete for the hand of Anne Reid (she later went on to play Val Barlow in *Coronation Street*) and I had to hit this sapling with an arrow. I'd never used a bow before and, although Richard Greene advised me, it was quite a long way off and only a small tree. The director said that if by some chance I did manage to hit it, I was to come back and say: "How about that?" But, miracle of miracles, I did hit it. I was so thrilled I went mad, shouting and cheering, instead of the controlled response. It was just a natural reaction. The only trouble with using that bow was it cut my arm to ribbons.

stage manager on a two-year course and Norman and I used to shift scenery because we were about the only ones who would stay up all night without moaning. But while I was there, I had all this fabulous training in things like fencing, country dancing and ballet.'

It was while he was with the Bristol Old Vic that Kenneth Cope made his television debut when cameras recorded a production of *The Duenna*. 'I played a fat old monk and was so padded up I looked like the Michelin tyre man. The whole school came to the dress rehearsal and nobody recognised me!'

Also at Bristol, he had his first experience of the supernatural, an early taste of what life would be like on *Randall & Hopkirk (deceased)*.

'I was charging up the stairs to make a quick costume change and I was suddenly aware of curious vibrations. I had the feeling that someone was coming down the stairs towards me, and I instinctively stepped out of the way. But there was noone to be seen. It was quite uncanny, but I was in too much of a hurry to think any more about it at the time. But I mentioned it later on to someone there, and it didn't seem to cause any surprise. I was told, quite casually, that it must have been Mrs. Siddons. The famous actress apparently still haunted the

'I also did an episode of *Ivanhoe* with Roger Moore. They asked whether I could ride a horse. With the usual actors' bluff, I said: "Of course I can." I'd been on a seaside donkey as a kid, that's all! Come filming, the girl groom introduced me to the horse. It was early morning, freezing cold and I was in tights. I got on the horse and it immediately reared up.

'She said: "Get off quick, it's got a sore back" and put me on another one. "Just walk it round."

'I didn't know what I was doing. I turned it and walked it down lots of long straight paths. Suddenly its ears went forward as it saw this straight and it was off – it thought it was on the gallops. My cloak was rigid in the breeze. We raced past where the rest of

the cast and crew were drinking hot soup. They looked on open-mouthed. I then proceeded to lose both stirrups and it was a mile before I managed to stop the beast. My legs were shaking with the sheer physical effort of gripping a horse with thin tights. I eventually trotted it back and the others said: "Jesus, Ken, we didn't know you could ride...".'

Another early television appearance was in *Dixon of Dock Green*. 'I played an army deserter who covered Jack Warner with a gun for half an hour. In the end, Jack said if I was going to shoot him, he wanted to die with his helmet on. He bent down to pick it up and as he did so, he pulled the carpet from underneath me and I toppled over. All the scenery shook. Although

It's not everyone who gets the chance to sit on their own head-stone. But then again, Marty Hopkirk isn't just anyone.

My dearly departed Chapter Two Gone but not forgotten

3. The Ghost Talks

the ending was a bit corny, I must say that Jack Warner was such a kind man. He went out of his way to give me advice – I learned a lot from him.

'Arthur Lowe was the same in *Coronation Street*. He played Leonard Swindley and he and I did a lot of funny scenes together. Jed – or Sunny Jim as he became known – had a stall on the market, selling bits and pieces, and people would actually write in and ask to buy the jumpers or whatever it was that week that I was selling. Jed's trademark was his peaked cap. I wore it to avoid typecasting, not to hide any baldness. It was my prop. As soon as I took it off, I lost Jed. I wouldn't have got *Randall & Hopkirk* if I hadn't worn a cap in *Coronation Street*. We had this lady director on the Street who tried to insist that Jed wouldn't wear his cap in bed. I refused to take it off – and got my own way.

'After I left, I saw a character in another Granada production wearing one of Jed's double-breasted suits. I rang the producer and said: "If ever you want me to come back, don't let anybody else wear my gear." Granada did want me to come back as Jed but the trouble was they kept offering me the old money!

'It was through *Coronation Street* that I got the chance to do *That Was The Week That Was* for the BBC in 1962. Granada heard about this and said: "You can't appear in both shows."

'I said: "All right, I'll do the BBC." It may have seemed a strange decision since Granada were paying me £250 a week, which was a lot of money in those days, and the BBC were paying me £50 just for a Saturday night live show. In the end, it didn't come to a choice because Granada relented and allowed me to do both.'

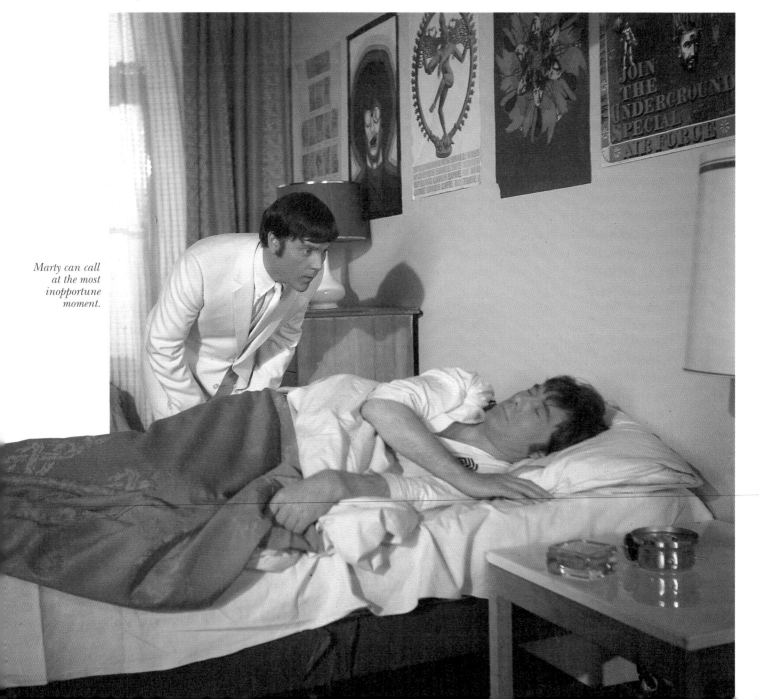

Marty can call at the most inopportune moment.

Since he was doing *Coronation Street* at the same time, *TW3* meant a hectic weekend. 'I used to catch a plane on Friday night, get home around 9 o'clock and a taxi driver or a motorcycle dispatch rider would arrive from the BBC with an hour-long script. I used to look at it and many times I'd just scream out of the room. It was quite hairy. It was all on autocue but autocue was very young in those days.

'I'll never forget the time that the floor manager took me to one side to tell me: "Kenny, you've lost the first two pages of your sketch and the last three. Good luck." The script had been ripping as it had passed through the autocue. Thankfully, I always had a script with me and as it was a kitchen sink sketch, I put the script in the sink and read it as I washed the dishes.

'Two things make me particularly proud about *TW3*. One, we had to come off because of a general election – no other show's had to do that; and two, West End restaurants had to have TV sets in their dining rooms, otherwise people wouldn't go out to eat.

'I didn't know any of the people in *TW3* before I worked with them, but soon discovered that our producer, Ned Sherrin, had great qualities of leadership. When the show went on the air, he made all of us feel like comrades going over the top together – to do or die. Mostly we did. It wasn't often we died.

'After the show, we used to go to a café in King's Road, Chelsea, to unwind. It was a very stimulating show to do and you tended to get a mixed reaction from the public. They either patted you on the back or hit you. Of course, Bernard Levin was actually attacked on the programme. I ran into him recently – it was good to see him.'

As a result of the success he was enjoying in two such high profile shows as *Coronation Street* and *That Was The Week That Was*, two more strings were soon added to Kenneth Cope's bow, those of pop star and disc jockey.

'Actor Harry Fowler was always playing practical jokes on me over the phone. So when it rang one day and the voice at the other end said: "We'd like you to make a record", I said, "All right, Harry, piss off." Except that this time it wasn't Harry, it was Tony Hatch!

'And so I did this record, which mainly came about because of the Jed Stone character, called *"Hands Off, Stop Mucking About"*. It got very high in the hospital charts! I got £46 in royalties from it.

Large by name, small by intellect. The Inspector demands an explanation in 'When Did You Start to Stop Seeing Things?'

'Soon after I was invited by Pye Records to do an evening show on Radio Luxembourg. I christened the show "Strictly for the Judys" ("Judys" was a Liverpool expression for girls) and I used to play my own record. I'd say: "Here's somebody who should go far – like Hong Kong..."

'I did two shows a week on Radio Luxembourg for a year. Sadly, I never did get to meet the legendary Horace Batchelor but I did know Keynsham. As a poor student, I had a houseboat there.'

Running parallel to his television career, Kenneth appeared in a number of films including *Yangtse Incident*, *The Lady Is A Square* and *Hammerhead*. 'I played a young officer in Dunkirk and if I hadn't been killed in that, John Mills would never have

'I was also in a couple of *Carry On* films – *Carry On At Your Convenience* and *Carry On Matron*. In *Carry On Matron* I played Sid James' son and he made me dress up as a woman. I had a wig in that too. I had to dress up in bra and suspenders and, long before Kenny Everett, I used to deliberately cross my legs on set in front of the cast. It would crease Terry Scott up – he had to leave the set.

starred in the film because it was he who took over the platoon from me.

'I was Omar Sharif's brother-in-law in *Genghis Khan* where I renewed my acquaintance with horses.

We filmed it in Yugoslavia and the horse they gave me to ride didn't understand a word of English. I had to do a scene riding through a wood, galloping along with armour on, a sword, a shield, and also carrying an important message. The scene was shot from a helicopter and for technical reasons to do with lighting, I had to ride with my right hand instead of my left, so I didn't have much control. What happened was that the horse saw the helicopter, became frightened and bolted like a mad thing between two enormous trees. I was lucky I wasn't killed. When the horse finally stopped, a groom came up to me and said: "Why did you go so far into the wood, Kenneth?" I felt like using my sword for real! And in the end, my epic ride was cut from the film anyway...

'They were circus horses and I soon found that if you whistled "The Blue Danube waltz" behind one of Michael Hordern's horses, it would sway from side to side. So I used to do this when all the animals were in a procession and it drove Robert Morley mad.

I used to totter along to the restaurant at Pinewood in my stiletto heels, calling into the gents en route. I remember one day this big coloured guy was in there. Then I came in and hitched up my skirt – he must have thought he'd got lucky!

'I often sat in the restaurant with Hattie Jacques, Kenny Williams and Joan Sims. Once, Ned Sherrin came in, the guy with whom I'd worked so closely for two years on *TW3*. There was I dressed as a woman and so in my best girl's voice I said: "Hello, Ned, how are you?"

'He did a circuit of the restaurant, came back and said: "Hello, Kenneth." But I'd got him for a second...'

Actors who have not had time to change out of costume are a familiar sight in any studio canteen. There is nothing quite like standing in the queue behind a *General Hospital* accident victim to put you off your lunch. Ken recalls a 1980 episode of *Doctor Who*: 'There was this poor actor playing one of the Tharils. We had a break for lunch on dress rehearsal day and he looked grotesque. There was no way he could take his make-up off, as it took him so long to put it on, and he wouldn't go to the restaurant because of his appearance. So I took him by the hand and forced him to come with me down the BBC corridors, up the lift, getting strange looks from the staff, to the restaurant. I almost had to feed him through his snout.'

Kenneth has also done a lot of writing over the years. 'And not just begging letters! Among other things, I've done episodes of *Village Hall*, the office comedy *The Squirrels* and *A Sharp Intake of Breath* which starred David Jason. And I put London Weekend Television on the air with a series called *Thingumybob* for Stanley Holloway. Paul McCartney did the theme music with the Black Dyke Mills Band. Unfortunately, the programme beforehand which was supposed to act as a trailer and explain the series, was blacked out and so when the opening titles came up and showed Stanley Holloway walking down the road with his dog, nobody knew what the hell was going on.

'Then I created a children's series for the BBC called *Striker,* about a kids' football team. I'm a devout Evertonian and my own sons, Mark and Nicholas, had just got into the boys' football team so I was able to write from experience. But the director didn't play football and the lead boy they'd got was a fisherman. I wrote a scene in which the ball came over in the air, the boy volleyed it into the net and the crusty old grandad who was watching, muttered: "He should have chested it down first." What you saw on screen was the ball going all the way along the ground and the boy hitting it into the net. Yet they still had grandad saying: "He should have chested it down first." It was crazy.'

Actor, pop star, disc jockey, horseman, writer, and some 20 years ago, restaurateur, when Kenneth and his actress wife, Renny Lister, bought premises in Watlington, Oxfordshire, and called it 'Martha's Kitchen' after their daughter. 'It was a tea shop turning over £25 a week when we bought it but it used to get packed with cabbies from London who came out for Sunday lunch. I don't know how they found out about it. We had a few famous diners too – Olivier, Terry Wogan, John Mortimer. The idea was that it would be an inheritance for the kids – like a big Italian family – but they've all gone and left me. The boys are in a band and Martha is starting out as an actress. We now own "L'Epicure" at Eynsham, a few miles west of Oxford, but Renny and I have leased it out.

'For the Girl Who Has Everything'. Marty makes sure that the only thing Jeannie takes down is shorthand.

My dearly departed Chapter Two Gone but not forgotten

3. The Ghost Talks

'I remember once we had a really toffee-nosed woman in the restaurant. She said to me haughtily: "I understand you are a television actor. What might I have seen you in?"

'"Well," I said, "I was in *That Was The Week That Was* and I was Jed Stone in *Coronation Street*."

'"I don't watch that."

'"I was the ghost in *Randall & Hopkirk (deceased)*"

'"I didn't watch that."

'"I was in the Co-op half an hour ago..."'

Although his TV appearances are less frequent than in the sixties and early seventies, Ken still pops

Compulsive gambler Aunt Clara consults her lucky numbers in 'The Ghost Who Saved the Bank at Monte Carlo'.

Marty demonstrates his ability to eavesdrop on private conversations in 'When Did You Start to Stop Seeing Things?'

up on screen from time to time. Among his recent roles was that of an eccentric millionaire in the series *Truckers*. 'He blew his money on women and drink. I asked for love bites on my neck!

'I always know when I've been on TV in a repeat the night before because the people in the village say hello and smile at me. The rest of the time they just ignore me. So I always know when to start looking out for repeat fees.

'In the wake of *Dunkirk, Genghis Khan* and *Randall & Hopkirk*, I've continued to die regularly. In fact, I've died twice in *Casualty* – once of a heart attack and once with a stomach complaint. There's not many people who can say that.

'I was also killed off in a 1967 science fiction film called *The Night Of The Big Heat*. I got killed by a monster after getting trapped under a car. When we were making it, we were reacting to a monster that we couldn't see at the time, cringeing back and looking terrified, but the producer had assured us: "You'll die

of fright at this monster." Then when we went to the first night at Edgware Road, we finally saw this terrifying creature. It was a sago pudding with an electric current in it. The audience just burst out laughing.

'Looking back on *Randall & Hopkirk*, it was a lovely series to make. Annette was a smashing girl and I remained great friends with Dennis Spooner. And Mike and myself remained firm friends right up until he died. He was such a nice, gentle guy to work with and while we were doing the show, we used to eat out together Friday or Saturday nights. Remembering what I had learned from people like Jack Warner, Mike and I used to go out of our way to help the guest actors, offering suggestions and general advice. We even had champagne on set to make them feel at home.

'And although I had a few run-ins with Monty Berman, all that's in the past. At a recent *Randall & Hopkirk* convention, I went up to Monty and put my arm around him. I swear there was a tear in his eye.'

My dearly departed Chapter Two Gone but not forgotten

Chapter Four
My Late, Lamented Friend & Partner
Mike Pratt

When Mike Pratt died of lung cancer on 10 July 1976, television lost one of its most familiar faces. Once described as having 'the weather-beaten looks of a mountainside which has been battered by the elements and can go on taking as much as nature cares to give', he had slugged his way to fame, either as hero or villain, in countless productions.

He tried to strangle Roger Moore in *The Saint*; gave Patrick McGoohan a sound beating in an episode of *Danger Man*; and was the villainous Simey in *The Adventures Of Black Beauty*. Yet this was also the man who composed that perennial children's favourite, 'Little White Bull', for Tommy Steele. Yes, Mike Pratt was respected by John Drake and Uncle Mac alike.

Born in London on 7 June 1931, the son of a journalist-turned-advertising man, Mike had always harboured dreams of becoming an actor. 'When I was 14, I wanted nothing more than to be an actor but, moving around at the end of the War, I lost sight of that.'

Instead he followed in his father's footsteps and worked for five years as an advertising copywriter. However he retained his interest in the theatre and landed a job as an assistant on a revue entitled 'Memories of Jolson' which introduced a young Shirley Bassey to the world at large. He admits: 'I never did discover what my primary task was supposed to be. I did all sorts of things backstage, the most important of which seemed to be to retrieve the musical director's false teeth, which he had a habit of taking out and

Jeff ponders how to get out of his latest predicament, designed by the Howarths (Peter Vaughan and Caroline Blakiston) in 'Never Trust a Ghost'.

Henry Foster (Alfred Burke) holds Jeff at gunpoint in 'All Work and No Pay'.

leaving around without being able to remember just where. I became his unofficial private eye – an early Jeff Randall – from the day I first found those missing molars for him.'

Sensing that the role of denture detective was unlikely to lead to a glittering theatrical career, Mike returned to advertising for a year although he combined it with a little part-time acting in minor roles.

A restless spirit, Mike decided it was time to see more of the world. So he quit the agency and, together with three friends, one of whom was Lionel Bart, 'bummed my way around Europe in an old taxi.' The quartet had clubbed together and bought the cab for £12. They then shipped it across to Scandinavia and embarked on an extremely rough guide of Europe.

Mike was also passionate about music. He was an accomplished jazz musician and on their return to London in 1956, Lionel Bart introduced him to another friend at a party – a young sailor named Tommy Hicks. Meeting a sailor at a party has led to the downfall of many a promising showbusiness career but for Mike, it was to be just the boost he needed. Tommy had a guitar and could sing, while Mike played the piano. They became firm friends and when Tommy was discovered by legendary promoter Larry Parnes (later nicknamed 'Mr. Parnes Shillings and Pence') at Soho's famous number 2 coffee bar, and left the Merchant Navy to become Tommy Steele, Mike collaborated with him on writing his songs. They formed a group called The Cave Men, named after The Cave, the run-down coffee bar which was one of their old haunts, and proceeded to play in pubs and coffee bars for ten shillings a night.

In the autumn of 1956 Mike was responsible for Tommy Steele's first hit, 'Rock With The Caveman', a little ditty which reached number 13 in the UK charts. Tommy's career exploded and he soon made a film based on his life, *The Tommy Steele Story*, for which Mike wrote the songs.

By then, Mike already had his own folk group, the Cotton Pickers. With Mike himself playing the piano and that indispensable instrument the washboard, the group picked up a number of club engagements and broadcasting dates. Meanwhile he continued to keep his hand in at acting, albeit still in walk-on roles.

Not seriously considering devoting his future entirely to acting, Mike's thoughts turned to writing and he went off to Spain to write a couple of plays which, many years later, had yet to see the light of day. Returning to Britain, he penned sketches and scripts for various revues and television shows as well as the story and songs for Tommy Steele's 1959 film, *The Duke Wore Jeans*. The following year, Tommy enjoyed his biggest movie success to date with *Tommy the Toreador*. Again Michael Pratt, as he was then known, composed the songs, including the catchy 'Little White Bull'.

A shortening of his name to Mike Pratt in the early sixties coincided with steady headway in his stage career. He graduated from the vast legion of unknown extras and found himself appearing in such films as *The Party's Over*, *Repulsion* and *This Is My Street*. In the latter production, made in 1963, he played Sid, June Ritchie's slovenly husband who 'eats in his vest and dries his face with the tea-cloth.' His pretty schoolteacher sister-in-law was played by a young Australian actress by the name of Annette André!

'I remember that film well,' says Annette. 'Ian Hendry and John Hurt were in it too. Mike was a lovely man to work with. He was the sort of guy who burned the candle at both ends – he enjoyed to work and play – and beneath that rough, wonderful face he was such a sweetheart. He was a marvellous actor and we had a lot of fun. I miss him very much.'

Standing 6ft. 1in. tall and with his rugged countenance, Mike discovered a lucrative line in playing villains in the many adventure series of the day. In addition to the treatment dished out to Messrs Moore

4. My Late, Lamented Friend & Partner

All's well that ends well:
Jeff waits to be rescued from the foot of a well in 'The Smile Behind the Veil'.

and McGoohan, as a hired hitman he murdered Patrick Wymark and shot Richard Johnson in the 1964 play '*A Question About Hell*'. Producers obviously also concluded that the Londoner could pass himself off as a foreign national. In two further episodes of *Danger Man*, he was cast as a Russian and a Bulgarian and again stepped behind the Iron Curtain for an episode of *Callan* in which he played a Russian diplomat. Most remarkable of all, in '*A Question About Hell*', Mike appeared as half-Negro. The make-up department must have been working overtime that night.

He played a car racketeer in *Gideon's Way*, a rebellious submarine engineer in *The Champions* and appeared in such popular series as *Redcap*, the military drama starring John Thaw, *No Hiding Place*, *The Man In Room 17*, *Court Martial* and *Market In Honey*

Lane. He even strayed to the right side of the law as a detective sergeant in an episode of *Man In A Suitcase*.

But it was *Randall & Hopkirk (deceased)* which propelled Mike Pratt to star status. Production finished in the late summer of 1969 and early the following year he was cast in an episode of Gerry Anderson's *U.F.O.* He then made a conscious decision to steer clear of television for a while and in May 1970 began a six month season of Shakespearean plays at London's Mermaid Theatre.

After his Shakespearean break, he threw himself back into television with a vengeance, playing a man who accidentally killed a hitchhiker in *The Expert* starring Marius Goring, and then a racing driver with marital problems in the Gerald Harper vehicle, *Hadleigh*. Still in 1971, he starred in Ian Curteis's

BBC2 trilogy *Long Voyage Out Of War* as army deserter Turk Godfray. The powerful plays, described by Mike Pratt as 'the most challenging and demanding role I have ever had to play', illustrated the effects of war during three stages of Godfray's life. The part required the actor to age from 21 to 56.

Monty Berman cast him once more in an episode of *Jason King* and in 1973 he appeared as Mordant, a 6th century Celtic horseman in the children's adventure series, *Arthur Of The Britons*.

In 1975, he portrayed alcoholic airline pilot Don Stacy in two episodes of the popular BBC family saga *The Brothers*. This was to be his final role. He had been ill for some time and was finally admitted to hospital in January 1976. Six months later, the battle against lung cancer proved one fight too many for Mike Pratt.

Although his appearance in *The Brothers* was a brief one, it attracted a sizeable following and in August 1976, one month after his death, the remaining cast of the series plus a number of other celebrities, including Glenda Jackson, John Le Mesurier and Kenneth Haigh, staged a special show in his honour at London's Aldwych Theatre. Proceeds went to his family.

As Kenneth Cope sums up: 'Michael was a great loss, both to the industry and as a friend.'

Jeff makes himself smarter than the police in 'Whoever Heard of a Ghost Dying'.

Chapter Five
For the Girl Who Has Everything
Annette André

It may come as a shock to her many fans but lovely Australian actress Annette André very nearly turned down the part of Jean Hopkirk.

'I believe I was considered for *The Champions*,' says Annette, 'but in the end they decided that Alexandra Bastedo would be better. So when *Randall & Hopkirk* came along, they offered that to me. Funnily enough, I didn't want to do it. I thought: "A series, oh no, I'll be typecast and ruined for television." But my agent said I should do it and some friends gave me the same advice so I relented. But I was a bit against it at first – I was a little worried. And to some extent my fears were justified because when the series ended, I couldn't find any work for a year.'

Annette is under no illusions about her role in the series. 'I was the standard pretty girl with smart clothes and legs. Those sorts of character were very stereotyped but luckily the series itself turned out not to be, which was wonderful. And Jean's part expanded as the series went on. Instead of just sitting about in the office, picking up phones, she was allowed to help with cases and become involved in the actual detective business.

'Unfortunately in those days, the girl in the series was always the lesser character in the producer's eyes. You were regarded as somehow being less important than the men. It was very unfair – it wouldn't happen now. But you were just the girl, a

selling point for the American market. Consequently, I didn't get to see the scripts early on. I wasn't really consulted although Ken and Mike were. Eventually though, I did work on the scripts with Ken and Mike to get more comedy put in. I think the production team were afraid of doing more comedy but without it, the show would not be as popular as it is today.

Annette André today.

'Somebody Just Walked Over My Grave'. Jeff announces that he's just seen the man who tampered with Marty's grave. Jean and funeral director Dighton (Bernard Kay) look suitably worried.

Even so, we all thought there could have been more comedy in *Randall & Hopkirk*.'

There may sometimes have been a dearth of amusement on screen but there was certainly no shortage on set. 'We used to have a terrific time,' says Annette, 'it would be quite hysterical. The three of us got on very well and there were a lot of practical jokes, a lot of laughs. I'm an awful "corpser" and Ken in particular would deliberately do things to make me laugh, to make me look at him. His favourite trick was to brush against my knee as he walked past. Since only Mike was ever allowed to react to him, that

would start me giggling and we'd have to do the scene all over again. I had a played a wife before several times but my husbands were always alive. It did make things rather easier.

'Ken was forever playing jokes on me. I remember going down to rehearsal one day, picking up my script and asking: "What scene are we doing? What are we on?"

'Ken replied such and such a page. All the crew were around, I opened the script and marking that page was a self-lubricating condom, which in those days was very risque!

In God we entrust Chapter Four

5. For the Girl Who Has Everything

'That condom got passed on. I used to play a lot of jokes on Roger Moore so I filled this wretched condom up with water and in the restaurant at lunchtime, put it on a plate with a silver cover. I had the waitress take it over to Roger who was having lunch with a group of very businesslike people. He took the silver cover off with a smile of delight and there was this lubricated condom filled with water rolling around on the plate. He looked across at me and knew instantly where it had come from.

'After putting the lid back, Roger passed it on to someone else and it proceeded to go through the whole of the restaurant and the whole of the bar. I remember Peter Wyngarde, who played Jason King, getting it at one point.

'But we did have a lot of fun. Department S were in the studio at the same time and Joel Fabiani, who played Stewart Sullivan, used to come over to our set to have a few laughs with us. He always thought it was much more fun than on his own set. And the crew were terrific. They would do anything for you and didn't pull the plug if we ran ten minutes over.'

Annette too remembers the set-swapping that used to prevail between rival productions. 'Whoever was taking over the library set would immediately re-dress it by putting in a couple of new books or changing a vase, just to make it look different.

'We had to be very good at doing scenes in one take. It became a standing joke when we'd see Monty Berman, bless him, on the set with his watch. I'd say, "It's got to be one take" and then Ken would do something so that there had to be a second take. Poor Monty would get very annoyed. We used to like to stir up the producer...'

When Annette landed the role of Jeannie, she was given an important piece of advice by Roger

Kenneth Cope fooling around off-set, much to the amusement of Annette.

Moore. 'He told me: "Now that you're doing a series, remember to concentrate on doing your own job. Don't try and do everybody else's. And the other thing is, if you want to throw a tantrum" – he knew I could be a little fiery – "only do it when it will mean something. And even then be sparing with your outbursts."

'So of course in the first few weeks I did everything Roger had told me not to. I threw myself into the job whole-heartedly. At the end of each take, I would race up the stairs to my dressing-room to get changed for the next scene. I became exhausted. And if, for some reason, something wasn't right – although it wasn't my fault or my problem – it became an issue.

'One day, I dashed upstairs for my usual quick change and found that not all of my costume was there. Blazing mad, I ran down to wardrobe and had this dreadful row with one of the wardrobe men. I shouted and screamed, he had a go back, and it was really nasty. I was in tears and moaning about everything. The situation between wardrobe and myself was somewhat strained for a few days.

'Then I remembered what Roger had said and I realised that I had been doing exactly the opposite. So the next time my clothes were incomplete, instead of running around like a mad thing, I calmly picked up the phone to wardrobe and politely asked whether they could bring the items up. And I apologised to the man with whom I'd had the argument. He apologised too and we became great friends after that. Similarly if the first director came into my dressing-room to ask, "Are you ready yet, Miss André?", instead of rushing, I began to pace myself. And I'd say: "Not just yet. A few more minutes."

'From then on, everything was fine. I had simply been too eager to get it all done. And I have followed that piece of advice from Roger Moore ever since.'

Like Kenneth Cope, Annette's main memory of location filming on *Randall & Hopkirk (deceased)* surrounds the regular excursions to graveyards. 'We spent an awful lot of time in graveyards,' she says ruefully, 'and it always seemed to be in winter. I nearly froze to death. To make matters worse, we only had one tiny caravan in which to sit between takes and for ages, it didn't even have a heater. That caravan was a monster – it was so small we could barely sit down. And we really had to kick up a fuss to get a heater.

'When I'm cold, I just cut off. I can't think of a thing – my mind goes. So I used to wear layers of clothing beneath what you'd see on screen. Inevitably of course, on top would be a lightweight dress because it was meant to be a different time of year. I'm sure a lot of the time I looked much fatter than I really was!

Jeannie trapped in the hall of mirrors with egghead Jansen (George Sewell) during 'Vendetta for a Dead Man'.

5. For the Girl Who Has Everything

'Alexandra Bastedo guested in one episode, "Whoever Heard Of A Ghost Dying?", and one night she and I had to have this fight in a graveyard. It was so cold and she had this pair of wonderfully warm mittens. On her last day of filming, she gave me the mittens to keep me warm through the rest of the series. I've still got them and I still wear them when I'm really cold.'

Despite the cold, Annette retains a warm feeling for Jeannie. 'She was a very nice woman with a bit of spark to her. She had a good sense of humour and clearly liked Jeff. I think had we gone on to do a

The graveyard brawl with Alexandra Bastedo in 'Whoever Heard of a Ghost Dying'

Whether or not it was an omen but in the years after playing a ghost's widow, Annette herself underwent several supernatural experiences. 'I do believe in ghosts and I think you have to be very, very careful with spirits because they can latch on. I've got a spirit in my London house who has caused a few problems. About eight years ago, before I was married, the house was divided into two flats. Some friends had come to live in the bottom flat and had obviously disturbed the spirit. I knew there was a spirit there – I used to hear the odd door closing – but she was fine. However she obviously didn't like the people moving in downstairs. I don't know what it was but it stirred her up.

'There were a number of incidents. A pair of slippers went missing, then turned up again at the place where they had last been seen about two months later. Then one day I was redecorating my part of the house – my mother was staying with me at the time – and I had made a pretty curtain, white with yellow flowers, for the kitchen window. I'd had to wait to get it put up over the weekend so I went downstairs to these friends and said to them: "Could you put these curtains on the spare bed?"

'They were carefully laid out. They were fine on the Saturday and on the Sunday my mother, my daughter and I and the people downstairs went off to a neighbour's for lunch. Because of my daughter, we came home early but the couple downstairs didn't get back until around 11pm. The next thing I knew there was a knock on the door and the woman downstairs said: "I hate to tell you this but there's some red wine on your curtains. I have no idea how it got there. We've just arrived home." I knew this was true because I had heard them.

'There were several red blotches, only on the plain white part, not the coloured bits, and they had not gone through to the lining. There were indentations which looked as if somebody had been up on the curtains, pressing on with their hand. But what was remarkable was that the door to the spare room had been locked all the time.

'I took the curtains to the cleaners but they couldn't shift the stains. I brought them home, thinking they would be for the rubbish bin. Earlier, I had done an experiment with removing red wine stains but I knew that this was not red wine – it was not the right colour. It was something that seemed to have been smudged on with a rag. Anyway, I made a weak solution of bleach and water and brushed on the curtain. As I did so, the stain just disappeared.

second series, we could have got plenty of mileage out of the relationship with Jeff. Of course, it could never have come to fruition – Marty would not have allowed that.

'I think my favourite episode was probably "The Ghost Who Saved The Bank At Monte Carlo", if only because it was meant to be set abroad which, even though it was all done in the studio at Elstree, at least gave us a feel of doing something different. Also, I was able to have glam hairstyles for that episode and wear evening dresses. So I rather liked that.'

5. For the Girl Who Has Everything

Jeannie relaxes in the South of Elstree for 'The Ghost Who Saved the Bank at Monte Carlo.'

'After that, I decided to get in touch with the psychic people as more odd things happened, often connected with sewing. She – the spirit – burned another pair of curtains.

'Then one day in July, I was in the kitchen talking to the psychic people about the possibility of them coming out to see for themselves and maybe exorcising the spirit when I became aware of this wind going around the room. I became very, very cold – and this was the middle of summer. It was almost a poltergeist, except that she didn't throw anything. The energy just whizzed around the kitchen – she was obviously very angry. But I talked to her a bit and said: "Calm down." And since then, she's been all right. She's still around and other people have told me they definitely think there's something there.

'I've had other strange things happen too. When my father died in Australia, he came by and said to me: "It's OK, I'm fine. I'm happy to be gone." And he touched my daughter Anouska at exactly the time that he was being buried in Australia. It was night-time here and she came in and woke me in bed. She was ice cold. It was his way of reaching out.'

Annette André has led a colourful, exciting life, one which in the past has seen her become something of a fixture in headlines and gossip columns. At one stage, she seemed to be in the papers almost as frequently as Andy Capp.

It all started in her native Australia. Her father was an Italian who emigrated to Australia, set up an upholstery business there and married a local girl. Young Annette's earliest wish was to be a ballerina. 'I

danced with the Australian Ballet Company but only for a very brief period because I was under age. I was 15 so they had to get rid of me quite quickly once they found out. Shortly after that, I decided I didn't want to be a ballet dancer any more and a nun at my school – I went to a convent in Sydney – suggested I do radio acting. This nun got me into radio school where you learned the technique of radio acting because radio in Australia was very strong then. There was no television in Australia. That didn't come until two years after I had started.'

Annette's bubbly personality made her a natural for comedy roles and she appeared with the likes of Bob Hope and Benny Hill when they toured Australia. As her career experience grew, she decided to expand her horizons. Encouraged by television producer Leslie Norman, who later directed three episodes of *Randall & Hopkirk*, Annette headed for Europe, arriving in Rome just as Elizabeth Taylor and Richard Burton were making the 1963 epic *Cleopatra*. If a girl had looks, an attractive figure and even the merest acquaintance with the acting world, there was a very strong chance of her getting into that mammoth production. Annette had everything plus, and thus made her movie debut as a handmaiden. 'It was such a small part I could hardly spot myself on screen!'

But the role did enable Annette to make contacts in the Italian film world, through one of which she appeared in an Italian-made production with Maurice Chevalier and via another she met British stage and TV producer Lionel Harris. About to make *Vanity Fair* on the London stage, Harris told Annette that if she decided to go on to England, he would willingly audition her for a part. She did just that, and made her British debut shortly afterwards in Harris's production. This in turn led to a television serial, *Emerald Street,* and the film with Mike Pratt, *This Is My Street.*

Before long, the petite actress, once described as being like a lemon sherbert on a hot summer's day – all blonde and cool – was in constant demand as a leading lady. *The Saint, The Baron, Sentimental Agent, The Avengers, Crane, Sergeant Cork, The Prisoner* – the list is endless. When Frank Ifield made his first starring film, *Up Jumped A Swagman,* it was Annette who was chosen to appear opposite him. In 1966, she was the only girl in *A Funny Thing Happened On The Way To The Forum,* in which she played Buster Keaton's daughter. 'He was a lovely old man,' recalls Annette. 'He'd sit down and say: "Where's my daughter? I want my daughter." Although he was on a ventilator and it turned out to be his last film, he was full of energy,

Jeff advises Jeannie to keep her head down in 'All Work and No Pay'.

'We could play musical chairs,' suggests Jeff to while away the time in 'When Did You Start to Stop Seeing Things?'

forever running on the spot. We were all in awe of him. I had a photograph taken with him but I never asked him to sign it, which I really regret now.'

Meanwhile Annette was furthering her reputation as a comics' foil, appearing alongside Dick Emery, Sid James and renewing acquaintances with Benny Hill. 'I was one of Benny's straight girls,' she says, 'an early Hill's Angel. He was a wonderful man, very shy and lonely and a bit eccentric.

'He actually proposed to me a long, long time ago. We went out a few times to restaurants in London and things like that. He suggested marriage. I can't remember what he said now. It was mentioned and then very gently not gone through with. There was never any big showdown or anything. He was fine about it, there was no problem. To me, he was a friend and that was it. Basically, I was too young at the time and my own career was

5. For the Girl Who Has Everything

starting. It just wasn't right, not the right combination. We had a good time, we had a lot of laughs together and he didn't feel he had to be funny all the time with me.

'Just a few years ago, my husband and I would watch Benny's shows in Los Angeles and laugh away. His death was very sad. When I heard he was ill, I telephoned the hospital in London. I hadn't been in touch with him for many, many years except for passing my regards on through other colleagues. He sounded very up and said he was feeling much better. I think he was a bit surprised to hear from me. It was voices from the past.'

Annette revelled in the Swinging Sixties. 'I loved living in London – I loved being able to get on a plane and be in a different country almost immediately. I suppose I was part of the jet set – parties in Chelsea, film roles and weekend trips to Europe.'

It was while filming *A Funny Thing Happened On The Way To The Forum* that Annette met legendary Spanish bullfighter El Cordobes. Their on-off relationship provided newspapermen with hundreds of inches of column copy but it was a case of mistaken identity which earned her the biggest headlines.

'It was at the time when George Best was leaving Manchester United and was always in the news. I knew George and had been out with him a couple of times and so when I saw him in a London nightclub one evening, I went over to him and said: "Hi, how are you?"

'But it wasn't me who left with him that night – it was somebody else – but I was the one who got in the national press as the mystery girl leaving the club with George Best.

'I woke up the next morning and the porter said: "For some reason, there are a lot of reporters outside. You seem to be in all the nationals."

'I was absolutely gobsmacked. It was all a mistake – it hadn't been me at all. However I got a lot of publicity out of it. I suppose at the time I thought it wasn't bad being on the front of the nationals – and they did choose a good photograph of me!

'As for George, we went out a few more times after that but it was nothing serious.'

'Vendetta for a Dead Man'. Jean gives Jansen the cold shoulder while cornered in the refrigeration plant.

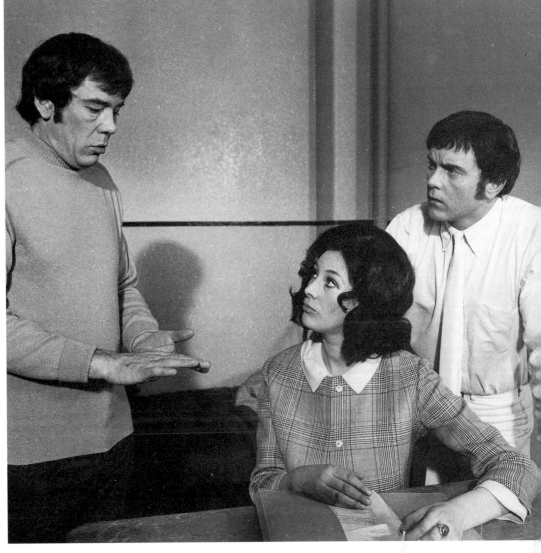

Annette André's former flatmate, Sue Lloyd, appeared as lawyer Elizabeth Saxon in the episode 'Money to Burn'.

In the wake of *Randall & Hopkirk (deceased)*, work was hard to come by for a time although Annette continued to make guest appearances in series like *The Persuaders* and *The Return Of The Saint* as well as embarking on provincial stage tours. The occasional lull resulted in the adoption of a new sideline. 'When I was out of work or not too busy, I designed capes. It started when I made myself a camel cloak. When friends saw it, they all wanted one. I never made any money from it but I enjoyed doing it.'

In 1984, Annette booked into the Crossroads Motel as Sarah Alexander, a ruthless businesswoman hell-bent on wrecking motel boss David Hunter's marriage. It gave her the chance to meet up again with Sue Lloyd with whom she once shared a flat.

Four years later, Annette appeared in the HTV production of *Maigret*, starring Richard Harris. 'I played Judith, a woman whose husband was murdered.' It was while working on Maigret that Annette first met the programme's American producer Arthur Weingarten whose impressive list of production credits includes *The Man From U.N.C.L.E.*, *The F.B.I.* and *The Bionic Woman*. He is also executive producer on the Granada *Maigret* series which stars Michael Gambon as the celebrated French sleuth. In 1989, Annette and Arthur married.

Besides family life, Annette's other great passion is animal welfare. 'I work as a volunteer with the Born Free Foundation for the Welfare of Wildlife, run by Virginia McKenna and Bill Travers, and I do talks in schools and clubs. I've always been interested in that area and while in America, I became involved with animal rescue. When I came over here, I went to a meeting where I met Virginia and Bill. I said to them: "There must be something I can do – if nothing else, I can talk." Now both Arthur and I work on a voluntary basis – he's mad about animals too. It's very close to my heart.

'I now tend to divide my life between London and Los Angeles although I haven't done much work in the U.S. At one point, I took three years off for myself. It was time I did that. Now I'm hoping to make something of a comeback.

'I still get recognised in the streets from *Randall & Hopkirk* and get a very good feedback from the public. It never occurred to me at the time we were making the series that it would be this successful so many years on. It was a great shame we didn't do another series. To my mind, they didn't do more because in those days, they used to try to sell series to the American network and if they didn't sell it (and virtually nothing did), it was then just disregarded. They'd say: "Don't spend any more time and money on that one." The show would be considered to be not very successful and stopped. *The Champions, The Baron, Department S, Jason King, The Persuaders* all only ran to one series. It was only really *The Saint, The Avengers* and later *The Protectors* which managed more. It was a pity because we had such wonderful ideas for a second batch. We wanted to go abroad, to take Marty overseas, to involve him in adventures with, say, a French ghost. That would have been fun.'

Chapter Six
The Man From Nowhere
Dennis Spooner

He wrote jokes for Harry Worth, scripts for *Coronation Street* and played football for Leyton Orient's third team. The late Dennis Spooner was a man of many talents yet the creator of *Randall & Hopkirk (deceased)* could scarcely have had a less promising start to life.

Born in Tottenham, North London, on 1 December 1932, Dennis never received a formal education. He attended school from 1941 but within a year had left to work for the Post Office as a telegram delivery boy, 'starting on a push bike and leaving on a motorbike.' Since his family were not evacuated during the Blitz, he grew up to the sound of exploding bombs and crumbling mortar. Further jobs followed – postman, clerk, window-cleaner, factory worker, would-be professional footballer – while at the same time he was making his first foray into showbusiness with Ralph Reader's Gang Shows, produced in the Mission Hall opposite Dennis's home. He performed with the Boy Scouts over a period of four years, the highlight being a Royal Command Performance.

Dennis's flair for comedy stood him in good stead when, at the age of 18, he was dispatched to Egypt as part of his National Service. Searching for any form of alternative to guard duty, Dennis volunteered to organise the entertainments. He tried his hand at stand-up comedy, proving so successful that the Forces Broadcasting Services recruited him to do a regular 15-minute Saturday show, gently satirising the week's news.

His National Service completed, Dennis returned to England and landed a job in London with the Railway, Mine and Plantation Equipment Company Ltd. It was as glamorous as it sounded but to relieve the monotony, he began submitting jokes for comedians appearing on the much-loved BBC radio series 'Workers' Playtime'.

With the sound of audience applause from fellow scouts and National Service colleagues still ringing in his ears, Dennis boldly ventured onto the stage as a solo comedian, touring pubs, clubs and music halls. In the pubs, he was about as popular as 'last orders'. On a good night, he was greeted with apathy. One night, he met a ventriloquist named Harry Illingworth who told Dennis that as a stand-up comic, he was a good gag writer.

Illingworth also underwent a change of direction, discarding his dummy and becoming bumbling comic Harry Worth. Dennis sold him material, usually for less than £10 a time, but when Worth made the transition to television, Spooner found that he could earn as much as £40 for a sketch. The financial lure of television proved irresistible and soon he was collaborating with Johnny Speight on sketches for 'The Arthur Haynes Show'. He also wrote a series called 'Tell It To The Marines' with John Junkin and another failed comic-turned-

The late Dennis Spooner.

'The Smile Behind the Veil'. Jeff has seen better days.

writer, Terry Nation, as well as contributing to the long-running radio show 'Life With The Lyons', starring real-life husband and wife Ben Lyon and Bebe Daniels.

It was at a party thrown by Johnny Speight that Dennis met a producer who was planning to turn one of Speight's scripts into a comedy film. His name was Gerry Anderson. In 1961, Dennis wrote nine stories for Anderson's latest creation, *Fireball XL5*, in addition to scripting episodes for the first year of ITV's new twice-weekly serial, *Coronation Street*. Mercifully Dennis's orderly mind ensured that there was no danger of Steve Zodiac joining Florrie Lindley in the Corner Shop or of Minnie Caldwell turning up in Space City.

That same year, Dennis was commissioned to work on another new series, *The Avengers*, following up with *No Hiding Place*, *Stingray* and *Hancock*. For the last-named series, Dennis and Richard Harris were thrown in at the deep end after the original writer was dropped. Tony Hancock was at his least co-operative and the result was not an enjoyable experience either for writer or viewer.

In 1964, Dennis joined the *Doctor Who* team, writing the historical story, 'The Reign of Terror'. He said it was the first of the Doctor's adventures 'to make deliberate use of humour. If you can introduce an element of humour through a specific character, then it suddenly becomes a marvellous way of padding the programme without boring the audience – the audience will always watch a funny bit and usually quite like it.'

Dennis then returned to the Gerry Anderson fold for *Thunderbirds*. 'I used to like writing for those puppet shows,' said Spooner later. 'You could do things in them that you couldn't do in other series. Up until that time, I'd always thought in terms of words but Gerry Anderson didn't really want a story.

'He always used to say: "Tell me four things that will look good on film."

'And you'd say: "A big fire...so on and so on."

'And he'd say: "Great."

'If you gave him the four things, which is what Hitchcock did, then the story became immaterial. And it was Gerry, more than anybody in this business, who taught me to think in terms of picture and add

6. The Man From Nowhere

Jeff discovers the body of Ramon Burgos Y Crackan in 'It's Supposed to be Thicker Than Water'.

the words afterwards, whereas before I worked with Gerry Anderson I'd always thought the pictures were of secondary importance. But of course he was right.'

After serving as script editor on *Doctor Who* for five months, Dennis wrote for *The Baron*. He then co-created *Man In A Suitcase* with Richard Harris and *The Champions* and *Department S* with Monty Berman. Jason King was one of Dennis Spooner's favourite characters. 'He was designed to be a total eccentric. He only ever turned up in *Department S* for ten minutes, but always had tremendous impact in that time. He was the only hero you did the most extraordinary things to. There was one episode where he knew that the crooks were going to be meeting at a warehouse, and he thought he'd catch them red-handed, so he had himself delivered to the warehouse in a wooden crate with champagne in, marked "FRAGILE" and "THIS SIDE UP". As it happened, he was delivered upside down, so he was hanging by the straps, and they loaded about 20 other crates on top of him. The police came and arrested the crooks and everything, and our hero had to be pulled out dirty, covered in champagne and straw, saying: "Which way did they go?" There was no other hero on television you could do that with because although he always had the answer right, it never quite worked out for him!'

Between *Department S* and the *Jason King* spin-off, Dennis created *Randall & Hopkirk (deceased)*. Regarding his role as script supervisor on this and other ITC shows, Dennis said: 'From finished script to post-production, it was totally in the hands of the director, and I

only became involved if there were problems – if the script was too long, too short, or something happened – because by the time they were on the floor shooting, I was dead worried about where the next script was coming from. It wasn't like working on a feature film or any one-off thing where you can start at the beginning and just literally go right through with no other thoughts, because there were other thoughts, and at that time ITC were turning out a lot of products and I got involved in other things.'

In 1972, Dennis Spooner and Monty Berman created their last series for ITC, *The Adventurer*, which starred Gene Barry as an actor-turned-spy. It was fraught with production and casting problems, the vast majority caused by the Americans' involvement. No fewer than five people had script control, including Barry himself and the sponsor's Chevrolet.

Right up until his death in September 1986 from a heart attack, Dennis continued to write delightfully offbeat stories for crime and detective series such as *Thriller*, *The New Avengers*, *The Professionals*, *Bergerac* and, in Hollywood, *Hart to Hart* and *Remington Steele*.

His former partner Monty Berman says: 'Dennis and I worked very closely together for ten years during which time we produced 150 hours of television. He was a man of immense talent and professionalism, and we became close personal friends. He had a natural touch – he just knew what to write for television. His fertile brain would produce brilliant ideas out of the blue. Quite simply, he seemed to know what audiences would want to watch. And that is a rare gift.'

Jeff struggles with the evil Lattimer (Keith Buckley) inside 'The House on Haunted Hill'.

Chapter Seven
Just for the Record
Complete Episode Guide
(Transmission dates and times refer to the London area)

1.
My Late, Lamented Friend and Partner
Sunday, 21 September 1969: 7.25 pm

Jeff Randall arrives at the home of Fay Sorrensen bearing gifts – photographs of her husband John's womanising. The blonde is still in bed but is only too happy to receive evidence which will enable her to obtain a divorce from her tycoon husband and wrest her father's business from him. That evening, she confronts Sorrensen with the photographs and announces her intention to file for divorce. She duly rings Jeff's office to request his presence at a meeting with her solicitor the following morning but Jeff is away and so Marty agrees to fill the breach. Meanwhile Sorrensen sneaks into his study and furtively makes arrangements over the telephone with what sounds suspiciously like a firm of contract killers.

The next morning, Marty arrives *chez* Sorrensen and parks his red Mini outside the house behind an electrician's van. With Mrs. Sorrensen still in the bath, Marty waits in the study. Suddenly he hears a scream from upstairs. Fay Sorrensen lies dead in the bath, an electric cable disappearing through a hole in the window to the electrician's van below. The van drives off and the doctor diagnoses a heart attack. Having assured himself of an alibi, Sorrensen returns home but is agitated to find Marty examining

Fay lies slumped in the bath.

the hole in the window and then talking to a group of children in the street. Their upward glance to the bathroom window convinces Sorrensen that his despicable ruse is about to be uncovered.

Jeff returns to the office to find Marty agonising over the accounts. When Jeannie rings, Marty promises to hurry home. He parks his Mini in the car park opposite their flat but as he crosses the road, is mown down by a black Humber saloon. Making his

John Sorrensen (Frank Windsor) prepares to go out, knowing that he has tightened the noose around wife Fay's neck.

getaway, the driver of the car is overpowered by a mysterious beatnik. Marty is dead.

In the wake of the funeral, Jeff starts receiving phone calls from a voice purporting to be Marty. Not surprisingly, he is somewhat sceptical but when he plays one of the recorded conversations back to Sid the night porter, Marty's voice is not on the tape. This, allied to the fact that Sid swears he has not put any calls through to the flat, convinces Jeff that Marty is for real.

At four in the morning, Jeff's flat window suddenly blows open and the curtains billow out. In a trance, he drives out to the cemetery where he comes

Marty visits the Sorrensen's household prior to his death.

face to face with the ghost of Marty, dressed in a white suit. Baffled and exasperated, Jeff exclaims: 'Why don't you stay dead like anyone else?'

Marty tells Jeff that he suspects Sorrensen is behind both killings but before he can elaborate, a distant bell heralds dawn. Marty recites an ancient rhyme:

'Afore the sun shall rise anew
Each ghost unto his grave must go.'

With that, Marty fades away to 'report in' but not before informing Jeff that he will be the only one able to see and hear him. 'You're the only one, Jeff. I chose you.'

Pursuing his inquiries, Jeff visits Happy Lee, a girl singer suspected of owning the car which felled Marty. She tells of an encounter with the beatnik, Hendy. After trailing Hendy, Jeff goes to Jeannie's flat where the ghostly spectre of a jealous Marty materialises once more. He chastises Jeff: 'You're making yourself at home, aren't you? Sitting there in my chair, with my slippers on. It's not showing proper respect. I'm not cold in my grave yet.'

The pair arrive at the seedy hotel where Hendy is staying and Jeff proposes that Marty uses his ghostly powers to get into Hendy's room.

'Glide through the wall,' he suggests.

'Glide?' says Marty.

Jeff is frustrated. 'What kind of a ghost are you?'

Eventually by concentrating, Marty passes through the wall and is able to warn Jeff that Hendy is lying in wait with a bottle. Marty creates further distractions by blowing up a storm, as a result of which he looks suitably pleased with himself. Hendy reveals the address of Marty's killer, who paid the beatnik £500 for his silence, but the assassin is found dead – gassed. Marty recognises him as the electrician outside Sorrensen's house.

Marty and Jeff set a trap, one which must be carried out immediately since Marty can only work at night. Jeff calls on Sorrensen and demands £25,000 to keep quiet about the killings. Sorrensen promptly alerts his hired hitmen. As dawn breaks, Marty panics and remembers some more of the rhyme:

'Cursed be the ghost who dares to stay
And face the awful light of day.'

He says he must go but Jeff persuades him to stay and help, if only for Jeannie's sake. The two private detectives follow Sorrensen who unwittingly leads them to the assassins. When they spot Jeff, they chase him in a car down a side street. Jeff runs for his life but just when all looks lost, Marty conjures up another gust of wind to blow a newspaper onto their windscreen. The driver loses control, the car crashes and the police arrive on the scene in cavalry-like fashion.

Back at the cemetery, Marty has been rejected by his grave because he did not return by daylight. He recalls the end of the rhyme:

'Ye shall not to the grave return
Until a hundred years be gone.'

So since he is stranded on Earth for the next 100 years, he offers to help Jeff with his future cases...and keep an eye on Jeannie.

Screenplay: Ralph Smart
Director: Cyril Frankel

CAST
John Sorrensen – Frank Windsor
Fay Sorrensen – Anne Sharp
Beatnik – Ronald Lacey
Night Porter – Harry Locke
Happy Lee – Dolores Mantez
Assassin – Harold Innocent
Electrician – Dave Carter
Hotel proprietor – Anthony Sagar
Detective – James Donnelly
Doctor – Tom Chatto
Manservant – Makki Marseilles

2.
A Disturbing Case
Sunday, 28 September 1969: 7.25 pm

Jeff's car is stolen and used in a curious robbery where a telephone call prompts a wealthy man to hand over all his valuables to a visitor. Meanwhile, unaware of her late husband's ghostly presence, Jeannie is puzzled when she and her sister Jennifer catch Jeff apparently talking to himself. Jeannie confesses that this unusual behaviour has been going on for some time.

The two girls decide to seek medical help and call in Dr. Conrad of the Lambert Clinic. They leave a tape recorder running in Jeff's office and when the tape is played back to the doctor, the evidence is conclusive. Jeff is rendered speechless and finds himself forcibly confined for treatment in the nursing home.

7. Just for the Record

Jean is comforted by sister Jennifer when Jeff seems to have disappeared.

After hearing Jean and Jennifer discussing Jeff's plight, Marty pays an unseen visit to the clinic and witnesses Conrad treating another patient, Leonard Whitty, with hypnosis in order to make him co-operate in robbing his own home. Marty conveys this information to Jeff, warning him to be careful, but Jeff, under similar hypnosis, merely reports it all back to Conrad. The malevolent medic realises he has a dangerously accurate case of extra-sensory perception on his hands and concludes that there is only one course of treatment – to edit the ghost of Marty right out of Jeff's mind.

Jean reluctantly consents to these measures with the result that Jeff's actions are now controlled by Conrad's voice alone. Sensing the gravity of the situation, Marty craftily mimics Conrad's voice, directs Jeff to escape and guides him to Whitty's house where another of Conrad's human robots, an ex-prisoner named Smart, is carrying out the robbery as planned. Marty (as Conrad) orders the hypnotised Jeff: 'The first man through that door, knock him cold.' Jeff lays out Smart's henchman accordingly but when the struggle continues, Marty instructs Jeff to become a karate expert. Announcing himself as Black Belt, Jeff leaps into action.

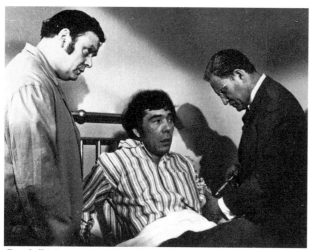

Randall tries to escape from the psychiatric ward but the sinister Dr. Conrad (David Bauer) puts him under sedation.

Meanwhile news of Jeff's escape has aroused the suspicious mind of Inspector Nelson, principally because no fewer than four robbery victims have each attended the Lambert Clinic. Thus the police finally decide to investigate the establishment and put an end to Conrad's lucrative little sideline.

Screenplay: Mike Pratt and Ian Wilson
Director: Ray Austin

CAST
Jennifer – Judith Arthy
Dr. Conrad – David Bauer
Dr. Lambert – Gerald Flood
Inspector Nelson – Michael Griffiths
Whitty – William Mervyn
Arthur Phillips – Charles Morgan
Smart – Patrick Jordan
The Sergeant – Adrian Ropes
First male nurse – Geoffrey Reed
Second male nurse – Max Faulkner
Hales – Les White

3. All Work and No Pay
Sunday, 5 October 1969: 7.25 pm

Not surprisingly, Jean Hopkirk is horrified when her furniture starts moving around her apartment faster than you can say 'Pickfords'. With furnishings and fittings flying in all directions, the spooky goings-on bear the hallmark of the work of a poltergeist. Scared out of her wits, she just manages to ring Jeff before the telephone is cut off. She rushes out into the street, the whole episode watched with considerable satisfaction by the oddball Foster brothers, Henry and George.

The Fosters' sombre, old-fashioned clothes make them look like undertakers and they drive off in their vintage Rolls-Royce as Jeff arrives on the scene. The fleeing Jean tumbles into Jeff's car and tells him what has happened, confiding: 'I've had this feeling for some time now...that Marty is trying to contact me.'

The conversation is overheard by the ever-watchful Marty who makes a desperate appeal to Jeff to assure Jeannie that she is wrong. But she remains convinced of Marty's presence and is therefore totally unsuspecting when the Foster brothers offer her a job. They claim to be spiritualists with a scientific approach who want to help her make contact with a loved one.

The invisible Marty accompanies her when she goes to the Fosters' country retreat where he is startled to hear Henry Foster tell Jean that a third spirit is present – the spirit of her husband – and that he is trying to get a message through to her. They promise Jean that they will use their psychic powers to contact Marty. Nevertheless, Marty is still sure that the pair are phoney.

Jeff pays £200 to enlist the aid of an alcoholic actress named Laura to approach the Fosters in the guise of a wealthy widow trying to trace a long-lost son, and persuades Jean to use her as a test case before accepting the job. From Jean's point of view, it seems a resonable idea since she will get commission for introducing a new client. Laura is supposed to pay Jean £200 for her efforts (thereby proving that she can still make decent money working for Jeff) but instead only gives her £25. Besides angering Jeff, the general outlook for Laura is bleak. The Fosters tell her that they are going to kill her and that when she reaches the other side, she is to contact Marty Hopkirk and bring him back to his wife.

Spotting a pile of Laura's clothes when they go to the old house to investigate, Marty and Jeff fear that the Fosters have carried out their deadly threat. They come to the conclusion that the Fosters have some crazy idea about making new spirits. Jeannie then arrives and it looks as though she and Jeff will be the next victims. They find themselves in the Fosters' bizarre chamber where the flick of a switch sends swords slicing within inches of their heads. Luckily, the ever-reliable Marty has made his way into a power station and, with intense concentration, he succeeds in blowing all the fuses over a wide area. The swords grind to a halt, allowing Jeff and Jeannie to escape. Making their way back to their car, who should they find on the back seat but Laura, wrapped in newspaper? She cheated death at the Fosters' hands by swimming across a lake, discarding her clothes in the process. She promises to pay back the £200 she owes Jeff but Marty confides: 'You don't want to believe everything you see in a newspaper, Jeff.'

Screenplay: Donald James
Director: Jeremy Summers

CAST
Henry Foster – Alfred Burke
George Foster –
   Dudley Foster
Laura – Adrienne Corri
Pawnbroker's clerk –
   Noel Davis
Man in laundromat –
   Michael Rathbone

4.
Never Trust
A Ghost

Sunday, 12 October 1969: 7.25 pm

Walking alone one night, Marty sees a man shot dead in his own home. He quickly alerts Jeff, giving a perfect description of the killer and even naming the dead man – James Howarth.

The police, in the guise of the irascible Inspector Clayton, visit the house to check out the story and Clayton is less than pleased when Howarth's wife Karen assures him that her husband is alive and well. The appearance of Howarth himself confirms this. To make matters worse, Howarth threatens to sue Jeff.

But Marty is still insistent that something strange is afoot and persuades Jeff to pay another visit to the house, ostensibly to apologise. Marty tags along too and while Jeff is talking to Karen Howarth, the ghost does some quiet exploring on his own. In the study, he comes across the killer – a man he later learns is called Rawlins. Excitedly, he warns Jeff but when the latter forces his way into the study, there is no sign of Rawlins.

By now, Jeff is thoroughly disillusioned with Marty, his mood not improved by a further complaint to the police from the Howarths and the threat of arrest from Clayton. Just when he is on the point of abandoning the case altogether, he receives a mystery phone call strongly advising him to do precisely that. This makes Jeff highly suspicious, all the more so when Marty reveals that there are two bodies in the Howarths' basement – those of James Howarth and his wife! The two people they have seen alive are imposters.

Jeff makes Sandra feel at home. Marty seems to approve.

7. Just for the Record

Jeff agrees to break into the house but the bodies have vanished and, worse still, he is caught in the act and reported to the police. He manages to escape and inveigles Jean into providing him with an alibi, even though it means her being found in a compromising situation with him when the police arrive. Convinced that Marty is suffering from hallucinations, Jeff approaches a ghost expert, Dr. Plevitt, who explains that ghosts exist in a fantasy world, populated by figments of their imaginations. He says the moral is simple: 'Never trust a ghost!'

So even when told by Marty that his life is in danger, Jeff pays little heed to the warning – until he receives an unfriendly visit from Rawlins. He realises that Marty has been right all along when he finds that Rawlins and 'Howarth' are framing him for murder. They explain that the real Howarth was in charge of salaries for British Intelligence agents and, as a result of his demise, they now possess microfilm detailing a complete list of agents' names and operating zones, information which would be potentially deadly in the wrong hands.

Marty contacts Plevitt and begs him to inform the police but the doctor refuses to act until Marty undergoes a special test to prove that he is not in a dream world. When Marty gets every answer right, the astounded Plevitt rings Scotland Yard as promised and the crooks are arrested in the nick of time.

Screenplay: Tony Williamson
Director: Leslie Norman

CAST
James Howarth – Peter Vaughan
Karen Howarth – Caroline Blakiston
Inspector Clayton – Donald Morley
Rawlins – Philip Madoc
Dr. Plevitt – Brian Oulton
Sandra – Edina Ronay

5. That's How Murder Snowballs

Sunday, 19 October 1969: 7.25 pm

On an evening out at the music hall, Jeff and Jeannie eagerly await the 'Russian roulette' part of a mind-reading double act. A member of the audience is asked to load the gun. One cartridge is live, the rest are blank. The routine has been performed over and over again but this time, the live cartridge is in the wrong chamber and the entertainer is shot dead in full view of the audience.

The victim's name is Fernandez and his partner Abel is immediately accused of turning the double act

Look at me when I'm talking to you.

into a solo venture. But Jeff is not sure that the desire for a bigger billing is sufficient motive for murder, particularly since he heard Fernandez's dying words: 'He said he would kill me...'

Who is 'he'? And who could have switched the bullets? The member of the audience who loaded the gun was a woman and she has mysteriously disappeared.

The resourceful Marty concocts a plan to enable Jeff to carry out his investigations at close quarters. Jeff goes along for an audition as a one-man mind-reading act which he successfully passes – with a little help from his ghostly friend. For when Jeff asks members of the audience to produce items from their pockets, like matchboxes, Marty relays the information to Jeff on stage.

'I've never seen a mind-reading act without an assistant before,' enthuses the man in charge of the auditions.

'True...true,' nods Marty, sitting in the seat behind.

When Jeff's act is finished, the man tells him: 'Yes...very good,' to which Marty replies indignantly: 'Good?...It's brilliant!'

Accepted as a replacement on the bill for the late Fernandez, Jeff is able to get to know the other members of the company, including the star of the show, singer Gloria Marsh, and choreographer Kim.

While searching the dead man's belongings in the theatre storeroom, Jeff is attacked, the only clue to his assailant being a brief glimpse of feminine legs. But his foray has one useful outcome. He has unearthed old newspaper cuttings which disclose that Gloria and Fernandez were married. Another clipping reports an accident in which Fernandez was exonerated from blame after the death of a man knocked down by his car.

Jeff quizzes Gloria and learns that her marriage to Fernandez was in name only. Despite his flings with several members of the chorus, Fernandez had continued to exercise a hold over her. He had refused to grant her a divorce and was blackmailing her since it was she who had been driving the death car prior to the accident. It also appears that Gloria and Kim are more than just good friends.

But before Jeff can make further headway, Gloria is battered to death. Then a stage hand is fatally stabbed after discovering a figure rummaging through the props. Finally, a girl dancer is attacked.

At their wits' end, the police re-enact the murder of Fernandez on stage. Abel is released from jail and reveals that he always positioned himself at the end of the seventh row. They realise that is where the killer must have been seated. Just then, a woman begins firing from the upper circle. A chase ensues during which the murderess is unmasked. It is not a woman at all – but Kim.

One of Jeff's more pleasurable assignments.

Screenplay: Ray Austin
Director: Paul Dickson

CAST
Gloria Marsh – Grazina Frame
Snowy – Arthur Brough
Barry Jones – Patrick Holt
Tony Lang – Harold Berens
Kay – Valerie Leon
Inspector Nelson – Michael Griffiths
Mark – James Belchamber
Fernandez – Tony Thawnton
Abel – David Jason
Kim – Stuart Hoyle
Old lady – Marie Makino
Doctor – John Cazabon
Ventriloquist – John Styles
Man with cards – Simon Barnes

6.
Just for the Record
Sunday, 26 October 1969: 7.25 pm

Jeff and Jean are engaged to act as escorts for contestants in an international beauty contest. Jean looks after Anne Soames, Miss London, while Jeff keeps an extremely close eye on Miss Moscow.

While Jeff is endeavouring to turn his duty into a romantic assignment, Jean wonders what there could possibly be in London to interest the entrant from

that city. To her surprise, and that of the watching Marty who needless to say has gone along for the ride, Anne Soames says that, rather unusually, she would like to visit the annexe of the Public Records Office.

Indeed the only person she meets there is a man named Pargiter, masquerading as a press

Partners in crime? Dorking, Anne Soames and Pargiter.

7. Just for the Record

photographer. It seems an unlikely setting for publicity shots and the mystery deepens when Marty sees Pargiter hand over a pair of spectacles for Anne Soames to hold when posing. But the glasses have a knife edge with which Anne promptly cuts the alarm cable system.

Realising that Anne is closely associated with Pargiter and that a crime of some sort is in production, Marty manages to prise Jeff away from his glam-orous charge to tell him what has happened. But since Jeff was unable to have witnessed the incident himself (indeed only an invisible ghost could), there seems little point in notifying the police. Instead Jeff goes to the hotel where the beauty queens are assembled and challenges Miss London directly. She responds by knocking him out, escaping and warning Pargiter and his two pea-brained henchmen, Dorking and Surrey.

Miss Moscow obviously felt the cold in London.

But she has seriously misjudged Pargiter and his motives for stealing documents from the Records Office. For the documents which Pargiter has been seeking are those which he believes will establish his rightful claim to the throne!

The exasperated Anne is subsequently tied up and held prisoner. Randall and Hopkirk eventually trace her and learn all about Pargiter's bizarre scheme. From then on, it is only a matter of time before they trump the would-be king.

Screenplay: Donald James
Director: Jeremy Summers

CAST
Pargiter – Ronald Radd
Anne Soames –
  Olivia Hamnett
Lord Dorking –
  Nosher Powell
Lord Surrey – Danny Green
Miss Moscow – Jan Rossini
Senior official –
  Michael Beint
Old man – Jack Woolgar
Miss Budapest –
  Kathja Wyeth
Attendant – Clifford Cox
Police Sergeant –
  Ken Watson
Photographer –
  Kevin Smith

Just hanging around. Anne Soames and a rather well-hidden Jeff hope Marty can rescue them from the warehouse fire at the end of 'Just for the Record'.

7.
Murder Ain't What it Used to Be!
Sunday, 2 November 1969: 7.25 pm

Paul Kirstner owes his wealth to years of racketeering in America. When the ageing gangster decides to visit his family in England, he gets a cold reception from his daughter, Susan, who has little time for a father who has neglected her for years and whose background she suspects. Even so, Kirstner starts to worry about her welfare when he discovers that he is still being harrassed by the smiling ghost of his late rival, Bugsy Spanio, who has been haunting him ever since

Kirstner engineered his earthly demise back in the Roaring Twenties.

Fearful of what Bugsy might do, Kirstner hires Jeff to protect Susan. But Bugsy is one step ahead and has already seen the opportunity to wreak a final revenge by exploiting the unique relationship between Jeff and Marty.

Marty's first inkling that something is amiss occurs when, not realising that Bugsy is also a ghost, he catches him with Jean in her bedroom. The jealous Marty is sure Jean is having an affair and protests violently to Jeff, telling him to do something about it. Jean is bewildered, a feeling shared by Jeff when he is unable to detect any sign of Bugsy in her company.

Marty finally realises that Bugsy is a fellow ghost when the gangster demands his help and says that

68

Jean will suffer if he fails to co-operate – 'I'm really gonna fix that dame of yours.'

So that he can keep guard on them, Jeff arranges for Jean and Susan to stay together. Meanwhile Marty feels intimidated by Bugsy whose greater experience in ghostly matters has given him a wider repertoire of tricks. It seems that the girls could be at Bugsy's mercy. As an added complication, Jeff, Jean and Susan are menaced by another of Kirstner's rivals (though this time a living one), a hoodlum named Lacey who is also hellbent on revenge.

With Lacey holding the trio at gunpoint, Kirstner approaches the house. Needing to create a diversion, Marty goads Bugsy into a ghostly fight by punching him in the stomach. Furniture starts flying everywhere and in the ensuing confusion, Kirstner succeeds in overpowering Lacey.

Bugsy teaches Marty new tricks.

It is when Kirstner plans to execute Lacey in the garden that Jeff realises that all the evil stories about Susan's father are true. But as Kirstner takes aim, he is distracted by the ghost of Bugsy wielding a white machine gun. Kirstner fires at the apparition, giving Lacey the opportunity to return fire to fatal effect. As Marty sums up before puffing on a celebratory cigar: 'So Bugsy got his man.'

Screenplay: Tony Williamson
Director: Jeremy Summers

CAST
Paul Kirstner – Alan Gifford
Bugsy Spanio – David Healy
Susan Kirstner – Sue Gerrard
Mrs. Maddox – Joyce Carey
Jack Lacey – Raymond Adamson
Harry – Patrick Connor
Hotel porter – Charles Lamb

8. Whoever Heard of a Ghost Dying?

Sunday, 9 November 1969: 7.25 pm

Jeff has made quite a name for himself as a result of his recent investigative exploits, his remarkable achievements not having gone unnoticed in the crim-inal world. One of its more perceptive members, a crook named Hellingworth, goes as far to suspect something supernatural and contacts clairvoyant Cecil Purley to confirm his theory. Purley is able to assure him that Jeff's late partner, Marty Hopkirk, is, in fact, still on earth in ghostly form.

Hellingworth and his girl confederate, Carol Latimer, put into action an astute plan to use Jeff and his invisible partner as fall guys in carrying out a series of large-scale robberies. By tricking Jeff into believing that he is being employed by an insurance company, they guess that he will persuade Marty to keep a close watch on a house Hellingworth says is suspected of being the meeting place of a gang which has been causing the insurance company so much trouble.

The ruse works. Marty overhears plans for the next robbery and reports to Jeff who in turn warns Inspector Large of Scotland Yard. Fed false information, the police keep watch. Of course, nothing happens – until the impatient lawmen depart, leaving the coast clear.

Further similar robberies follow but the crooks know that sooner or later they will have to remove Marty from the scene so that he will never be able to reveal the truth. And the only way to do away with a ghost is to have him exorcised.

Purley's treatment is a slow process and the unfortunate Marty suffers all the pangs of human illness. Jean is drawn into the murky affair when

Marty discovers that exorcise isn't always good for you.

Purley (Charles Lloyd Pack) recoils in horror.

Carol Latimer approaches her and says that her late husband needs her assistance because he is earth-bound. Some of his personal possessions are required to help Purley carry out the exorcism at Marty's grave.

Marty fights hard to save himself, promising: 'I'll get you for this, Purley, if it takes me the rest of my death!' His last link with mortality is becoming very slender by the time Jeff arrives on the scene, knowing that he somehow has to save Marty if he is going to save himself from a lot of trouble with the irate Inspector Large, who is already accusing him of being involved in the robberies.

Screenplay: Tony Williamson
Director: Ray Austin

CAST
Hellingworth – John Fraser
Carol Latimer – Alexandra Bastedo
Inspector Large – Ivor Dean
Cecil Purley – Charles Lloyd Pack
Doctor – Richard Caldicot
The butler – Peter Hughes
Lord Manning – John Richmond
Ray – Romo Gorrara
Pete – Terry Plummer
Larry – Paddy Ryan
Constable – Robin John
Second Constable – Philip Weston

9.
The House on Haunted Hill

Sunday, 16 November 1969: 7.25 pm

Jeff finds himself struggling to cope with two cases at the same time when delving into a diamond robbery as well as the mystery of a haunted house.

Rumours abound that Merston Manor is haunted and so Henry Mace Horsfall and Frederick P. Waller are summoned to investigate. Although dressed in a tweed frock-coat and deerstalker like a Sherlock Holmes clone, Waller's credentials for the task appear somewhat fragile when he beats a hasty retreat from the mansion after hearing strange noises. Since the house's reputation is making it difficult to sell, a real estate agent named Webster searches for someone made of sterner stuff and approaches Jeff for help. Preoccupied with the gems investigation, Jeff decides that Webster's request is definitely a job for Marty – an instance of mixing your spirits.

Looking into the disappearance of the consignment of diamonds, Jeff receives a telephone call urging him to visit a warehouse where he will learn something of importance. Walter Previss is waiting for him there. He is a member of the firm concerned and offers to do a deal with Jeff if Randall will issue a report stating that it was not an inside job. Being a man of principle, Jeff flatly refuses.

Meanwhile Marty's progress is hindered by the fact that he too is scared stiff of the goings-on at Merston Manor. Even a ghost can take fright in a haunted house! And Marty is convinced that the building is in the grip of the supernatural – until Jeannie's sister Jennifer, who is working as Jeff's secretary in Jean's absence, is abducted and traced by Jeff to Merston Manor. Previss and his vicious side-kick Lattimer are holding her there as a hostage to force Jeff's hand. It becomes clear that the house is the headquarters of the gang which carried out the robbery and that its reputation for being haunted has been cleverly contrived over a long period.

After following Jennifer there, Jeff is quickly overpowered. Only Marty can be relied upon to fetch help but as he points out despairingly: 'Who's going to listen to a ghost giving them directions to a haunted house?'

As luck would have it, a public meeting is being staged locally that night to discount the existence of a ghost at the Manor. Among those present are Waller and Horsfall. Marty finds himself able to communicate with Horsfall and relates that there will be a double murder at the house tonight. A cast of thousands descend upon the Manor and Jeff and Jennifer are rescued, proving conclusively that a man-made ghost is no match for the real thing.

This eerie figure (in reality Lattimer) endeavours to frighten Jeff off the case.

Lattimer threatens the hapless Jennifer.

Screenplay: Tony Williamson
Director: Ray Austin

CAST
Jennifer – Judith Arthy
Walter Previss – Jeremy Burnham
Frederick P. Waller – Peter Jones
Henry Mace Horsfall – Dermot Kelly
Langford – Duncan Lamont
Lattimer – Keith Buckley
Webster – George A. Cooper
Carlson – Garfield Morgan
Colonel Jarrett – William Kendall
Miss James – Carol Rachelle
Smith – David Sinclair
Simpson – John Kidd
Jackson – Terry Duggan

10.
When Did You Start to Stop Seeing Things?

Sunday, 23 November 1969: 7.25 pm

The day when Jeff can no longer see or hear Marty is the day both have been dreading. And now it seems to have arrived. Worse still, Jeff does not seem bothered by it – he appears to have forgotten all about Marty. Thinking this curious behaviour might be due to overwork, Marty attends a psychiatric session conducted by the celebrated Sir Oliver Norenton and takes advantage of a patient's hypnotic state to convey Jeff's address to Sir Oliver.

The work in which Jeff has been engaged is that of finding out who has been leaking information from the Towler Corporation and using it to play the Stock Market. The police, represented by Inspector Large, are also taking a keen interest because one of

7. Just for the Record

Laker and the fake Jeff. The likeness is remarkable...

the directors, Tully, was murdered after arranging an appointment with Jeff.

Marty then hears Jeff ring up Holly, the company's personnel manager, to fix an appointment. Holly is later found dead but Jeff swears to Large that he never made the call. Marty is thoroughly perplexed. Using another of Sir Oliver's patients, a Mrs. Trotter, Marty again tries to jog Jeff's memory with a message but Jeff dismisses her quickly because he is hiding a shady character by the name of Jarvis with whom he seems to be in cahoots. Then, after making plans with Jarvis, Jeff gains entrance to the apartment of the firm's Managing Director, Hepple, and kills him – despite Marty's gallant attempts at intervention.

By now, Marty is ready to believe the worst of his partner until, back at Jeff's apartment, it finally dawns on him exactly what has been going on. For there he sees 'Jeff' remove a cunningly applied face mask to reveal somebody else altogether, a man named Hinch.

Inspector Large is certain that Randall is involved in the murders but the excuse given by Hinch (disguised as Jeff) is that Hepple gave him the case in the first place, so why should he want to kill him? But then Jean remembers that it was the General Manager, James Laker, who gave Jeff the case and not Hepple.

Independently of course, Jean and Marty head for Laker's house where Marty finds the real Jeff locked in a cellar.

Jeff: 'What've you been up to all this time? OK, so he's a good double but I thought you were supposed to be psychic.'

Marty: 'He happens to be very good. He was bad-tempered, just like you, he's not very bright, just like you, and makes the usual number of mistakes...'

Jeff: '...Just like me.'

With a little help from Marty, Jeff floors Jarvis, only to be laid low himself by a blow from a mace wielded by Jean who, unaware of the existence of the imposter, remains under the impression that Jeff is a murderer. She soon realises the error of her ways with the arrival of Laker and Hinch (in mask) who hold her and the real Jeff captive while Laker reveals details of his Stock Market killings.

The only hope of rescue lies with Sir Oliver. So when Sir Oliver hypnotises himself, Marty seizes the opportunity to plant certain ideas in his head – namely that he should go to Laker's house and that he is a secret agent, licensed to kill. Acting accordingly, Sir Oliver bursts in on Laker and his cohorts and in the ensuing confusion, Jarvis mistakenly shoots the fake Jeff instead of the real one. At that point, Inspector Large makes his customary late entrance.

Screenplay: Tony Williamson
Director: Jeremy Summers

Another day, another body, for Inspector Large and his team.

CAST
Inspector Large – Ivor Dean
Sir Oliver Norenton – Clifford Evans
Jarvis – Keith Barron
James Laker – Reginald Marsh
Mrs. Trotter – Bessie Love
Hepple – Basil Dignam
Holly – Philip James
Tully – John Garvin
Hinch – David Downer
Sir Timothy Grange – Peter Stephens
Diana – Rosemary Donnelly
Tilvers – David Stoll

11.
The Ghost Who Saved the Bank at Monte Carlo

Sunday, 30 November 1969: 7.25 pm

Marty's Aunt Clara is an inveterate gambler. Since the death of her husband, she has been perfecting her winning system in the casinos of London and, having won her air fare, is now ready to tackle the big one – Monte Carlo. Sensing that she might need protection while making her fortune, she plans to hire her nephew but, on learning of his death, opts for Jeff and Jean instead.

Despite efforts to change her mind, she insists on proceeding with the expedition and so Jeff and Jean accompany her, joined by a worried Marty. For one who looks more at home at a Women's Institute whist drive, Clara proves amazingly successful. She wins a considerable amount of money on her first night in Monte Carlo, much to the interest of rival racketeers Lawsey and Sagran. Intrigued by her exploits in London, Lawsey has gone so far as to follow her out to Monaco.

Both men are determined to lay their thieving hands on Aunt Clara's little red book which contains all her figures, and minor gang warfare breaks out between the pair. For her part, Aunt Clara is offered protection by the casino manager, Tapiro, which is just as well since Jeff falls down badly on the job when succumbing to the wiles of a glamorous girl named Suzanne who seems to have been employed by Sagran to get him out of the way.

Marty tries his luck at the gaming tables.

7. Just for the Record

Fortunately, Marty is more vigilant although even he is unable to prevent the little red book from being stolen. Aunt Clara is unperturbed. She says the figures mean nothing – the secret of her system is in her head.

As she goes on winning without the book, it appears highly likely that Lawsey and Sagran will switch their attentions to regaining the money, thereby placing her in greater danger. The only way to save her is to force her to lose, and that is where Marty comes into his own. The racketeers, by now working in collusion, retire in disgust.

Ironically, Aunt Clara's sacrifice seems to have been unnecessary since Tapiro had matters under control and Suzanne is not what she appeared to be. It looks as though a fortune has been lost but the intrepid Aunt Clara has other ideas...

Screenplay: Tony Williamson
Director: Jeremy Summers

CAST
Clara Faringham – Mary Merrall
Lawsey – Brian Blessed
Suzanne – Veronica Carlson
Sagran – John Sharp
Tapiro – Roger Delgado
Max – Nicholas Courtney
Terry – Roger Croucher
André – Nicholas Chagrin
Claude – Clive Cazes
Verrier – Michael Forrest
Hibert – Hans De Vries
French croupier – Colin Vancao
Young lady – Eva Enger
Hotel receptionist – Richard Pescud
Bell boy – Christopher Eedy

12.
For the Girl Who Has Everything
Sunday, 7 December 1969: 7.25 pm

Complaining to his spiritual partner about lack of finances, Jeff senses that help could be at hand when he receives a visit from ghost hunter James McAllister who reveals that he has been employed by millionairess Kim Wentworth to look into the ghostly haunting of Crake Castle. McAllister is by no means certain that the ghost is genuine but since he singularly fails to detect the presence of Marty, his competence is open to question. Nevertheless Jeff accepts McAllister's offer to share the £1500 fee.

Events take a startling turn when Kim, awoken by the clanking of chains, is confronted by a sinister hooded figure at midnight. By the time her screams alert McAllister, the figure has vanished. In the circumstances, Kim is less than pleased when her seventh and latest husband, Larry, informs her that he is going to his artist's studio the following night, thus leaving her alone in the castle. McAllister suggests that Jeff should follow Larry Wentworth who is tailed to a cottage where he is seen silhouetted with another woman. When Jeff and Marty return to the castle, they find McAllister slumped dead in a chair.

The evidence could point to a ghost, both Kim and her French manservant, Jean-Claude, being adamant that nobody had entered the castle. But Jeff and Marty discover that someone could easily have been hidden in an old priesthole concealed behind a bookcase. And Marty makes another interesting find when learning that Mrs. Pleasance, who runs the village tea shop, The Buttery, is psychic. She can actually see and talk to him. She also operates a curious line in home electrics.

Two nights later, Jeff, keeping guard at the castle, is roused by Kim's screams and the sound of a gun firing. He arrives to find the body of Larry Wentworth, shot by Kim, after apparently trying to attack her.

This appears to be a tragic conclusion to the case. Larry Wentworth has obviously invented the

Fancy waking up next to that...

Unmasked, Jean-Claude looks much more appealing to Kim Wentworth.

priesthole where she plans to leave him to rot. It transpires that Kim intends to fly to Rio with Jean-Claude after the inquest prior to making him husband number eight.

Only Marty knows of Jeff's predicament. In desperation, he remembers Mrs. Pleasance. He tells her to go to the castle and open the priesthole, enabling Jeff to arrive at the inquest just in time to reveal the truth about Kim and Jean-Claude.

Back in the office, Marty celebrates the fact that he can now contact anyone via Mrs. Pleasance. But at that moment, the lady in question turns up in white, having fallen prey to her own eccentric electrics. Back to the drawing board, then, for Marty.

Screenplay: Donald James
Director: Cyril Frankel

CAST
Kim Wentworth – Lois Maxwell
Mrs. Pleasance – Marjorie Rhodes
James McAllister – Freddie Jones
Larry Wentworth – Michael Coles
Jean-Claude – Paul Bertoya
Laura Slade – Carol Cleveland
Vicar – Eric Dodson
Girl – Carol Dilworth
Police Sergeant – George Lee
Coroner – Basil Clarke

ghost in order to frighten his wife and then get rid of her in order that he can inherit her fortune and marry Laura Slade, the girl at the cottage. But Jeff is not satisfied. He knows that Larry could not have killed McAllister. He vows to continue with the case, refusing Kim's proposal of a pay-off.

At midnight, Jeff is disturbed by the hooded figure emerging from the shadows. In the struggle the 'ghost' flees to Kim's room and reveals himself as Jean-Claude. His attempts to clamber into the priesthole are thwarted by Marty who blows the curtains of the four-poster bed to ensnare him. Jeff moves in for the capture but is felled by Kim. He topples into the

Marty hitches along for the ride with Elliot.

13.
But What a Sweet Little Room
Sunday, 14 December 1969: 7.25 pm

Following the heartbreak of losing her beloved husband, wealthy widow Anne Fenwick believes she has found happiness with handsome, aristocratic Arthur de Crecy, known to his friends as 'Bunny'. He takes her to a quiet country cottage and she immediately falls in love with the lounge – a sweet little room. But her joy turns to horror when she discovers that 'Bunny' has

Jean-Claude and Jeff do battle.

De Crecy and Elliot discuss tactics.

7. Just for the Record

locked her in with gas hissing up from the floor. As she gasps for breath in her desperate attempts to escape, she can see 'Bunny' in the garden digging a grave: her grave.

Business is slack for Randall and Hopkirk, Marty being reduced to conducting office demonstrations of his ghostly ability to make cups and saucers rattle. But then work finally arrives in the shape of Julia Fenwick who wants Jeff to trace her missing aunt, Anne. Unaware that his every move is being watched, Jeff learns that Anne had been attending seances held by one Madame Hanska. Jeff poses as Anne's nephew but is unable to elicit any information of worth from the Madame who accuses him of being a sceptic.

The investigation takes on a more sinister tone when Julia, having been dropped off by Jeff at her mews home, is run over and killed by De Crecy's servant, Rawlings, who covers his tracks by depositing a drunken salesman at the wheel. The key to the case appears to be Madame Hanska and so Jeff arranges for Jeannie to attend one of the seances, using an assumed name, Mrs. Ramsay, and asking whether she can contact her dead husband, John. The ever-protective Marty disapproves but in vain. The medium is unsuccessful at contacting 'John' but after the meeting, Jeannie is comforted by a Mr. Elliot who begins asking questions about her mythical ex-spouse. Jeannie thinks Elliot is innocuous but Marty is not so sure and spirits his way into the man's flat where he hears him relaying the details of 'John Ramsay' over the phone to Madame Hanska. At the next seance, Madame Hanska miraculously makes contact with 'John'. The message comes through that he is worried about Jeannie's finances and wants her to call on his old friend, Arthur de Crecy.

Jeannie duly visits de Crecy whose offer to look into her financial situation is withdrawn when he realises that she and Jeff are private eyes. De Crecy arranges for Jeff to be beaten up by Rawlings and Elliot. Jeff is warned to stay away from Madame Hanska.

The instruction does not apply to Marty however and at the next seance, he appears as a vision to Madame Hanska. He tells her she that she has psychic powers which she must not abuse whereupon the old phoney is so stunned that she reveals all about the scam with de Crecy – how she is paid commissions for sending rich widows to him. Acting on this, Jeff forces de Crecy to take him to where Anne Fenwick is 'staying'. De Crecy leads him to the country cottage and asks him to wait in the lounge. History begins to repeat itself as Jeff finds himself trapped with gas seeping into the room. The quick-thinking Marty tells Jeff to light an oil lamp and hide in a trunk, at which the ghost succeeds in toppling

the lamp, thereby causing an almighty explosion. De Crecy, digging a new grave, rushes back to investigate. Held at gunpoint by Jeff, who has stepped unharmed from the trunk, de Crecy is forced to confess all.

Screenplay: Ralph Smart
Director: Roy Ward Baker

CAST
Arthur de Crecy – Michael Goodliffe
Madame Hanska – Doris Hare
Elliot – Norman Bird
Julia Fenwick – Anne De Vigier
Anne Fenwick – Frances Bennett
Rawlings – Raymond Young
Salesman – Chris Gannon
Andrews – Cyril Renison
Martha – Betty Woolfe
Police Inspector – Joby Blanshard

14. Who Killed Cock Robin?
Sunday, 21 December 1969: 7.25 pm

Jeff Randall as always had an eye for the birds – but not necessarily the feathered kind. So an assignment to act as guardian to an aviary of tropical birds leaves him somewhat puzzled. Nevertheless he accepts the offer made by a lawyer named Laverick who explains that the birds are part of the £2 million estate left by the eccentric Mrs. Wentworth Howe. Under the terms of her will, the entire estate is left in trust for as long as the birds live – probably 20 years or more – and it will not be until all birds are dead that the estate will be divided among the surviving relatives. As can be seen, the late Mrs. Wentworth Howe was a few grains short of a sprig of millet.

Jeff questions Sandra Joyce while Marty lends an ear.

Attempts have already been made to shoot the birds, suspicion focusing on the occupants of the Wentworth mansion – Colonel Chalmers, James Howe and his wife Gabrielle, and niece Sandra Joyce, the rebel of the family. The aviary is being looked after by the gamekeeper, Beeches.

Beeches (David Lodge) in menacing mood.

Jeff's arrival is greeted with barely-concealed hostility and he is grateful for the services of Marty who can keep watch on the aviary without being seen. But the pair are unable to forestall a human killing when James Howe is found dead in the aviary – poisoned. And there is further evidence that somebody had tried to kill the birds too. Gabrielle believes her husband must have gone there to save the birds but she is determined to have them eliminated and endeavours to set fire to the aviary. She is foiled by the invisible Marty who is, however, powerless to prevent her from becoming the second murder victim.

The finger of suspicion is now pointed firmly in the direction of Beeches yet he is the only one who does not stand to gain anything from either the deaths of the humans or the birds. Meanwhile it is learned that a hired assassin, Gimbal, has been engaged to kill off the birds but before he can name his employer, he too meets an untimely end.

The cause of the deaths is found to be by way of a dart dipped in a poison obtainable in India. Colonel Chalmers comes under the spotlight when it is revealed that he spent much of his career in India. But before he can be challenged about the sorry business, he also is killed.

In the midst of the murderous mayhem, Laverick arrives at the mansion, staggered by what is happening and realising that there is now only one legatee – the lovely Sandra. Marty is of the opinion that she could be behind the foul play but Jeff and Laverick plump for Beeches who has already been detained and released by the police. After the latest killing, Jeff and Laverick decide to lock him in the wine cellar until the police can interview him again. But that theory receives something of a setback when Beeches becomes the next casualty.

That leaves only Sandra but before he can turn his attention to her, Jeff is knocked unconscious by Laverick and incarcerated in the cellar. Sandra is left alone with the scheming Laverick and there is just one man who can help her – Marty. But what can a ghost do? The answer is to get a message to his widow, Jeannie, who is at a party where some of her friends are holding a seance with an upturned wine glass. They receive the shock of their lives when they contact a real ghost.

Screenplay: Tony Williamson
Director: Roy Ward Baker

CAST
Laverick – Cyril Luckham
Sandra Joyce – Jane Merrow
Mrs. Howe – Gabrielle Brune
Beeches – David Lodge
Colonel Chalmers – Maurice Hedley
James Howe – Tenniel Evans
Gimbal – Michael Goldie
Police Sergeant – David Webb
Johns – Philip Lennard
Carol – Susan Broderick
Peter – Leslie Schofield

Another one bites the dust.

15. The Man From Nowhere

Sunday, 28 December 1969: 7.25 pm

Jean Hopkirk is stunned to find a highly presentable young man in her apartment, one who proceeds to make himself very much at home. She is even more amazed when he claims to be the reincarnation of her late husband, Marty.

Whoever he is, this new Marty has been extremely thorough with his homework. He appears to know all about Marty's past, right down to his personal habits. To the alarm of Jeff and the ghostly Marty, the imposter is so convincing that it seems as though Jean is beginning to believe that his claims are true. She starts to see more and more of him.

Jeff manages to take a photograph of the new Marty, and the old model, brooding over it, is sure that he has seen the man somewhere before. Two other men are also taking a keen interest in the ripening relationship between Jean and the imposter – Hyde Watson and Mannering. This odd couple turn up in all manner of guises in a bid to keep tabs on Jean and 'Marty'.

The real Marty is becoming increasingly concerned that his successor in Jean's affections is aiming to take his place as her husband. But the presence of Hyde Watson and Mannering suggests something altogether more sinister than a simple desire for matrimony, especially when they abduct the 'reincarnated' Marty who however, with Jeff's assistance, succeeds in escaping.

The compliant Jean, virtually certain that the new man in her life really is Marty, agrees to go with him to a village in Oxfordshire where they had spent the first night of their honeymoon. The real Marty and Jeff are able to discover their whereabouts as, indeed, are Hyde Watson and Mannering. For it transpires that a thug called Griggs and the man claiming to be Marty are fully aware that Jean is the only person who can lead them to the precise spot where they hurriedly buried stolen treasure following a collision with Jean and her bridegroom on the first day of their honeymoon. After that crash, 'Marty' lost his memory and now needs

Jean to direct him to the burial place. But the villains' plans are wrecked when the spectral Marty finds a novel way of calming Griggs' menacing dogs.

Screenplay: Donald James
Director: Robert Tronson

CAST
'Marty' – Ray Brooks
Hyde Watson – Michael Gwynn
Mannering – Patrick Newell
Griggs – Neil McCarthy
Mullet – James Bree

16. When the Spirit Moves You

Friday, 2 January 1970: 7.30 pm

Jeff is approached by one Calvin P. Bream who claims to be a New York detective requiring a bodyguard. He fears becoming an endangered species after putting the word around in London that he is trying to recover some negotiable bonds stolen from a client of his in New York.

But in truth, Bream is no detective. He is a con man who has double-crossed a client named Cranley and his associate Corri by offering them an unlimited supply of fake bearer bonds. Now to put them off the scent, Bream is insisting that he is only the middle man. He names the top dog as Jeff Randall. And Bream needs all the help he can get for he has sadly miscalculated in his attempts to sell counterfeit bonds to Corri, who turns out to be a big-time criminal, unlikely to take too kindly to being duped.

Curiously, when Bream has too much to drink, he can see and hear Marty through his drunken stupor. Consequently, Marty discovers that Bream has placed Jeff in grave peril. And Bream actually confesses that should Cranley and Corri realise that they have been conned, they will kill him. Cranley and Corri have already declared their intentions by planting a murdered man in Bream's hotel room. Yet it is Jeff who is caught by his old adversary, Inspector Large, with the body, whereupon Bream, Jeff's only alibi,

Jeff has a quiet word with the landlord (James Bree).

denies ever having seen him before.

Not for the first time, Marty comes to Jeff's rescue. He knows that the only way to communicate with Bream is to get him drunk and once under the influence of alcohol, Bream becomes terrified of Marty's ghostly presence. Marty warns Bream that unless he tells the truth, he will haunt him and materialise 'night after night after night.' Bream is well and truly hooked. He admits to the police that he had lied but Large, feeling cheated of his prize catch, threatens further action against Jeff unless he can bring in the bigger fish within a couple of days.

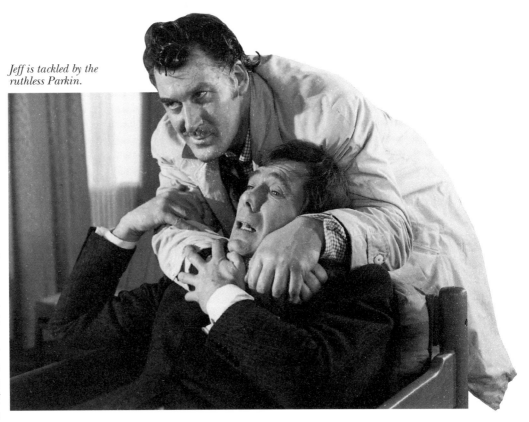

Jeff is tackled by the ruthless Parkin.

Cranley and Corri have £125,000 in hot money which they can only get out of the country by means of bearer bonds. And they still think that Jeff and Bream have the bonds. Corri tells Jeff that he has 24 hours to fetch the elusive bonds or, 'I'll kill you – not personally, of course, but just as surely as if I pulled the trigger.'

Kidnapped by Corri's henchmen Perrin and Wilks, Bream plans another con trick to fool the enemy into believing that the bonds really do exist. They are to be deposited in the night safe of Corri's bank while simultaneously the £125,000 is placed in the night safe of Jeff's bank. But Perrin intercepts the bonds and when Corri sees they are worthless, he sets out to recover his money and blow Jeff to oblivion at the same time. Using the expertise of a seasoned safe-cracker named Manny, Corri breaks into the bank and forces Jeff to sit in a chair, a foot or so from where the safe door is about to explode. Beforehand, Corri takes the precaution of making sure that Jeff's fingerprints are all over the vault. Bream is in hiding and Marty knows the only way to persuade him to act on Jeff's behalf is get him drunk and threaten him with further hauntings. Sure enough, Bream is panicked into phoning the police who arrive with impeccable timing.

'Getting to be quite a villain, aren't you, Randall?' says Large. 'First murder and then armed robbery.'

'You don't expect to be able to prove a word of that,' replies Jeff. 'Do you...?'

'No,' admits Large. 'I just wanted to see your face when I said it.'

Screenplay: Tony Williamson
Director: Ray Austin

CAST
Inspector Large – Ivor Dean
Miklos Corri – Kieron Moore
Calvin P. Bream – Anton Rodgers
Perrin – Michael Gothard
Wilks – Peter Jay Elliott
Manny – Reg Lye
Cranley – Anthony Marlowe
Plain clothes Police Sergeant – Richard Kerley
Girl in luxury flat – Penny Brahms
Parkin – Bill Reed

Bream attempts to explain his position to gangster Miklos Corri.

17.
Somebody Just Walked Over My Grave

Friday, 9 January 1970: 7.30 pm

Horrified to find his own grave being desecrated one night, Marty summons Jeff to investigate. Randall arrives in time to see a man in eighteenth-century costume, complete with breeches, stockings and buckled shoes.

Even by Jeff's standards, this is decidedly unusual and the next day, determined to prove that the period vision was not merely a figment of his imagination, he goes along to the funeral parlour to see whether there is a logical explanation. The director, Dighton, denies that any work was done near Marty's grave on the night in question but while Dighton is in conversation with Jean, Jeff catches sight of the man in costume. He gives chase but is knocked out for his pains.

On coming round, he finds himself in the company of a man named Mandrake who takes him to nearby Mandrake Hall to patch his wounds. The man freely admits to being a fake. He had bought the residence and the title, changing his name to Mandrake, but his 20-year-old son, Harry, an agrophobic hippie painter, has proved a bitter disappointment to him. For Harry is in no fit state to carry on the refounded dynasty and is living the life of a hermit in the basement of the house.

Jeff rejects Mandrake's offer of a sizeable sum of money to turn Harry into a suitable heir. But on the way out, he recognises Harper the gardener as the man in the historical costume.

Finding the police on his tail, Jeff has a change of heart and decides to accept the case in order to lie low. Under cover of darkness, he begins to take a closer look at the greenhouse and he and Marty find the entrance to an underground passage, one end of which leads to Marty's grave, the other to Harry's bedroom. But Harry is conspicuous by his absence. He has been abducted and it becomes apparent that the period costume was intended to unnerve anyone who caught sight of the abductors in the preparation of their plot.

A fast-travelling hearse with Dighton, Harper and a coffin inside gives a fair indication of the kidnappers' identity but since marks on Harry's bedroom wall imply that he gave them inside help, Mandrake decides against paying any ransom. Instead Mandrake reveals his intention to marry Martha, his miniskirted housekeeper, in the hope of producing a more desirable heir.

Realising that his plot to hold himself to ransom has failed miserably, Harry can do nothing as Mandrake marries Martha. After the wedding, Marty muses: 'I wonder what happened to Harry?' The answer is revealed. Harry is earning his living as a fairground freak, billed as the man who lives underground.

Screenplay: Donald James
Director: Cyril Frankel

CAST
Mandrake – George Murcell
Dighton – Bernard Kay
Martha – Patricia Haines
Harry – Nigel Terry
Harper – Geoffrey Hughes
Dr. Cholmond – Cyril Shaps
Valerie – Beverly Winn
Commentator – Andrew Sachs
German commentator –
    Michael Sheard

*Mandrake (right)
decides his son Harry
is an unsuitable heir.
Or did he mean hair?*

18.
Could You Recognise the Man Again?

Friday, 16 January 1970: 7.30 pm

Leaving a New Year's party, Jeff and Jean catch a man coming out of their car. They believe him when he says he mistook their car for his own – until they find a dead body in the boot.

The corpse is that of a protection racketeer named Jennings. Inspector Large, acting with unaccustomed perception, is quick to link the murder with a long-standing feud between Jennings and rival gangsters George and Mort Roden. It appears an open and shut case when Jeff and Jean positively identify George Roden as the man they saw leaving their car.

George is subsequently arrested but his mother, the brains behind her sons' racketeering, is not unduly perturbed. She is confident that the family's crooked lawyer, Ralph Sorrel, will be able to win an acquittal...provided, of course, that Jeff and Jean can be prevented from giving evidence.

So she wastes no time in arranging for Jean to be removed from the action and held captive by Mort and another thug, Hales. The case against George Roden thus hinges entirely on Jeff who, after listen-

Unaccustomed as he is to public cooking, Jeff asks Marty for a second opinion. Yes, it's definitely an egg.

ing to the abducted Jean's voice on the telephone, is made fully aware that his evidence will not only convict Roden but seriously damage Jean's health.

Jeff decides not to give evidence until he has found the star witness. The case is adjourned until the following day, leaving Jeff and Marty a matter of hours to trace the missing Jean. Being a worried ex-spouse, Marty has naturally tried to track down Jeannie from the moment she first disappeared but has been puzzled by the fact that her aura repeatedly leads him back to her apartment. Yet she is certainly not there.

Scouring London for the Rodens' secret hideout, Jeff ends up back at Jean's apartment with Marty. The search has proved fruitless. In just 15 minutes, George Roden will walk free through lack of evidence. As a last-ditch effort, Jeff urges Marty to think of Jeannie while he is in her apartment. Marty finds himself levitating towards the ceiling and returns to ground level with the feeling that Jeannie had just walked across his grave. Realising he is on to something, he passes through the ceiling into the flat above where, indeed, the Rodens are holding Jeannie.

Her release effected, there remains the problem of getting her to the court in time but Marty manages to throw a spanner into the judicial works by blowing the court papers around, thus causing a delay. Jeff and Jean arrive on cue, forcing a rueful Roden to change his murder plea to guilty.

Mort Roden (Dudley Sutton) abducts Jeannie.

7. Just for the Record

Screenplay: Donald James
Director: Jeremy Summers

CAST

Inspector Large – Ivor Dean
Mrs. Roden – Madge Ryan
George Roden – Stanley Meadows
Mort Roden – Dudley Sutton
Mike Hales – Norman Eshley
Ralph Sorrel – John Bryans
Jennings – Roland Curram
The Judge – A.J. Brown
Prosecuting Counsel – John Harvey
Sgt. Hinds – Richard Kerley
Loftus – Billy Milton
Tina – Tricia Chapman
Ben Craddock – Dudley Jones
Tramp – Walter Sparrow
Shop assistant – David Cargill
Harry – Michael Gover
Uniformed Inspector – John Arnatt
Chalmers – Bruce Beeby

19. A Sentimental Journey

Friday, 23 January 1970: 7.30 pm

Rummaging around for a pair of socks one morning, Jeff's search is interrupted by a warning from Marty that he is about to receive two visitors. Two men promptly march into Jeff's flat uninvited, search the place and fell the occupant with a blow to the stomach when he has the audacity to ask what is going on. Then two more men arrive, smart and business-like – unknown to Jeff, they are gangland bosses Seymour and Hamilton. They offer Jeff a job to escort a courier carrying an item worth £10,000 from Glasgow to London on the night express. The item must be handed over to Seymour in London and a receipt taken back to Hamilton in Glasgow. Highly suspicious, Jeff refuses. But a further beating brings about a change of heart and he reluctantly agrees to act as chaperone for £200.

Jeff arrives at the given address in Glasgow, part of a seedy tenement block. Entering the dingy flat of Mr. Alexander, he is pleasantly surprised to find that the courier is an attractive blonde who goes by the name of Dandy Garrison. She has an attache case chained to her wrist.

On the journey south, Jeff spots that they are being shadowed by two men. Learning that people have been enquiring as to which sleeper cabins he and Dandy have booked, Jeff asks Marty to keep watch on the girl through the night. This looks like being one of Marty's more agreeable assignments. However Jeff is soon woken by an agitated Marty, announcing that Dandy's cabin has been broken into. The culprit, one of the mysterious men in the buffet car, reveals himself to be Detective Sergeant Watts of Glasgow Police. He asks Dandy to open the case but it contains nothing more than a selection of lingerie. How could it be worth £10,000? It is only when Watts has departed that

Tony appears to hold the advantage over Jeff.

Dandy discloses that she herself is the valuable item.

Thoroughly confused by the whole business, Jeff soon finds that there is another shock in store for him. For as they reach Seymour's London gymnasium and the crook fetches the receipt envelope from his safe, the lights suddenly fuse, allowing Dandy to make a run for it. In a panic, Jeff grabs the envelope, his escape abetted by Marty who conjures up a sandstorm to ward off pursuers.

Now a much sought-after property himself, Jeff seeks out Dandy. Marty tracks her down to an exclusive London hotel where Jeff discovers that she is in league with one of Seymour's men, Tony. In a scuffle, Jeff loses the receipt to the couple and is knocked unconscious. Tony then rings Hamilton to report that Jeff has stolen the receipt.

Under pressure from Seymour to find the double-dealing duo, Jeff meets up with Watts

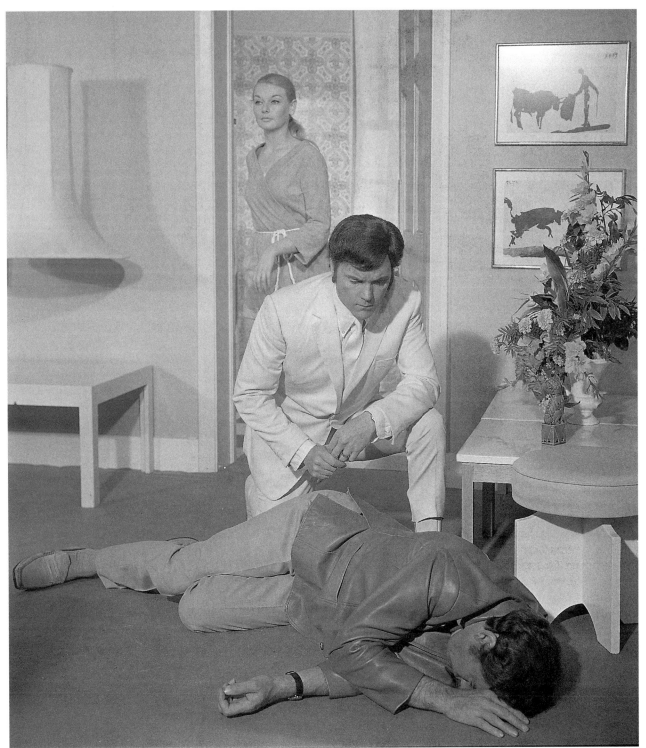

Marty find Jeff in a familiar position.

Marty plans to foil Dandy's plot.

who finally begins to make sense of the curious caper. He realises that the stamp on the receipt must be one of two rare stamps stolen recently from the Laxton Philately Company and worth £10,000. But where is the other? The answer comes courtesy of a visit to Seymour's gymnasium. Jeff is attracted by a pocket watch hanging prominently from Seymour's waistcoat. Hidden inside is the second stamp.

Meanwhile, Dandy and Tony have made their escape in Seymour's limousine, joined by Marty as an invisible passenger. The wily wench tricks Tony into checking the rear of the car and seizes the opportunity to drive off with the stamp – and Marty. The ghost gets Jeff to call the car phone and when Dandy takes it off the hook to stop it ringing, he is able to relay their route to Jeff. Watts realises they are heading for an airfield where Seymour has a private plane but Dandy's getaway is thwarted at the last minute by Marty blowing the craft into motion. Stranded on the runway, Dandy is easy prey for Watts and his men.

Screenplay: Donald James
Director: Leslie Norman

CAST
Sam Seymour – William Squire
Dandy Garrison – Tracey Crisp
Tony – Drewe Henley
Det. Sgt. Watts – Victor Maddern
Hamilton – Antony Baird
Alexander – John Rae
Man in phone booth – Larry Taylor
Sleeping car attendant – Michael Bird
Albert – Billy Cornelius

20.
Money to Burn
Friday, 30 January 1970: 7.30 pm

Tempted by the prospect of making some easy money for a change, Jeff is intrigued by a proposition from an old friend, Kevin O'Malley, who offers to cut him in on a plot to hijack banknotes which are about to be withdrawn from circulation and are en route to the incinerator. Since Jeff's cut would amount to a cool £500,000, it is something to which he gives a great deal of thought.

But Randall is wary. He knows the opportunist O'Malley is as slippery as a plate of jellied eels and suspects that the only reason he has been invited in on the job is so that he can be used in some way as a fall guy. O'Malley leaves the matter open, saying that he can be contacted through Anne-Marie Benson at a London club where he is working on a cabaret act with her and another girl, Angela Kendon. Having said that, O'Malley stresses that time is at a premium – the notes are to be burned in the Battersea Power Station furnaces the following evening.

The plot is uncovered when a mishap reveals that old newsprint, instead of the notes, is going into the furnace. The police are alerted about the switch, the prime suspect being Jeff whose car was spotted in the vicinity of the power station at the time. With the scent of blood in his nostrils, Inspector Large builds up what seems a water-tight case against Jeff whose only alibi is Anne-Marie. He claims to have been dining with her at the time his car was seen but she denies all knowledge of his very existence. To tighten the noose around his neck, some of the missing money is found in Jeff's apartment.

Marty fears for his partner's future, a feeling shared by Jeff's glamorous lawyer, Elizabeth Saxon, particularly when she discovers that he really had been at the power station, and not with Anne-Marie.

Anne-Marie refutes Jeff's alibi to Inspector Large.

7. Just for the Record

His excuse was one of simple curiosity. O'Malley is puzzled too. For he had lost his nerve and had not even attempted to go through with the theft. So who did? He believes in Jeff's innocence which leaves just

Marty stows away on board a plane to thwart Anne-Marie and Angela Kendon.

one other person who knew about the plan – Anne-Marie. Unfortunately, O'Malley unravels the mystery just too late to prevent Anne-Marie and Angela Kendon completing their escape. They have their own plane and are safely in the air bound for the Continent, unaware however that they are carrying excess baggage in the form of Marty. Once again, it is down to Marty alone to rescue Jeff from a seemingly hopeless predicament.

Screenplay: Donald James
Director: Ray Austin

CAST
Inspector Large – Ivor Dean
Elizabeth Saxon – Sue Lloyd
Kevin O'Malley – Roy Desmond
Anne-Marie Benson – Linda Cole
Angela Kendon – Olga Lowe
Sgt. Hinds – Richard Kerley
Policeman – Norman Beaton
Chemist – John Glyn-Jones
Bank worker – John Hughes
Security man – Tom Bowman
Uniformed policeman – Roger Avon
Choreographer – Don Vernon

Angela Kendon, supported by Anne-Marie, points a gun at O'Malley after he has discovered that they were responsible for the robbery.

21.
The Ghost Talks
Friday, 6 February 1970: 7.30 pm

Lying in a hospital bed with an arm and a leg in plaster after falling from a balcony while trying to apprehend a safe-breaker, Jeff reluctantly finds himself acting as a captive audience for the garrulous Marty. The latter sees the opportunity to recount the tale of a case he handled successfully before his death – a matter of national importance, the full details of

7. Just for the Record

In happier times: Marty locked in a moment of passion with Jeannie.

which he had never previously revealed. So Jeff is forced to listen disbelievingly as Marty basks in his erstwhile glory.

It all began with a telephone call to the office asking for Jeff. Since Jeff was out of town at the time, Marty answered and accepted it for what it claimed to be – a call from Sir Basil Duggan, the deputy head of M.I.5. He met the man who said he was Sir Basil at a military club and agreed to undertake a vital espionage mission, to recover essential documents stolen by a counter-spy. Enlisting the help of professional safe-cracker Joe Hudson, Marty carried out his instructions and stole the papers from a private house, only to learn later that he had broken into the home of M.I.5 chief, Major General Hickson. For Marty had been blissfully unaware that 'Sir Basil' was himself a counter-spy, named Brenan.

In desperation, Marty tracked down Sir Basil and, naturally enough, found that this was not the man who had hired him. The only solution was to trace the masquerading Major Brenan. In doing so, he unwittingly succeeded in putting Jeannie's life at risk when another member of the spy ring, Parker, appeared on the scene, intent on silencing Marty for good. The listening Jeff sympathised...

Fortunately, says Marty, he had taken the precaution, as all good detectives should, of jotting down the fake Sir Basil's car number. He was thus able to unearth Brenan's address and to follow him to the docks where, with courage and initiative beyond the call of duty, he brilliantly halted the spy's escape and brought the case to a triumphant close.

Jeff, who had done his best to interrupt throughout, is mightily relieved at finally being able to rest his eardrums. Just then, Jean enters the hospital. She has been thinking about Marty and has decided to tell Jeff all about the time Marty successfully tackled a spy case single-handed...

Screenplay: Gerald Kelsey
Director: Cyril Frankel

CAST
Major Brenan –
    Alan MacNaughtan
Jackson – John Collin
Joe Hudson – Jack MacGowran
Parker – James Culliford
Chief Inspector Horner –
    Thomas Heathcote
Captain Rashid – Marne Maitland
Sir Basil Duggan – Geoffrey King
Long – Peter Cellier
First man in steamroom –
    Hilary Wontner
Second man in steamroom –
    Jack Lambert
Dr. Musgrove – John Boxer
Groves – Martin Carrol
Page boy – Ian Butler

Horner and Hudson have just told Jean that they want Marty in connection with a robbery.

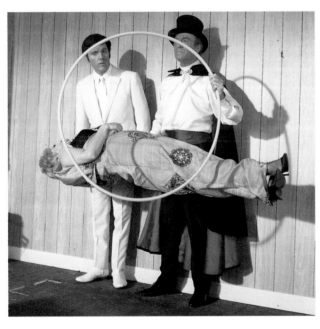

22.
It's Supposed to be Thicker Than Water
Friday, 13 February 1970: 7.30 pm

Jeff is hired by Joshua Crackan and his solicitor, Hodder, to deliver an envelope to Joshua's nephew, escaped convict Johnny Crackan. It contains a letter inviting surviving members of the Crackan clan to a reunion, ostensibly to celebrate Joshua's 80th birthday.

The task seems routine enough and, after tracking down Johnny, Jeff returns to Joshua to collect the £50 he was promised. He is immediately offered further work to act as a guard at the party and allow in only those with invitations. This causes friction with Marty who resents Jeff telling him not to interfere for once and to leave him alone for a while.

The far-flung Crackans assemble for the party. Together they make a veritable United Nations – there's the Rev. Henry Crackan from America; Ramon Burgos y Crackan who is rumoured to have Spanish blood; the Chinese Sung Lee Crackan; and blonde Fay Crackan, a magician's assistant.

But the event turns out to be infinitely more sinister than a family get-together. One by one, the guests die in mysterious circumstances – first Ramon, then Johnny, followed by Sung Lee and the Rev. Henry, leaving only Fay, who wisely chooses to make her exit before she can become the next victim.

Fay's reprieve could be merely temporary, however, as Joshua admits that it is only by removing all his relatives that his estate can pass to his loyal employee, Hodder, whom he wishes to be his heir.

Although in her line of work, one would expect Fay to be adept at disappearing, she faces a tough opponent in Hodder who is hot on her trail. Meanwhile Joshua has taken steps to ensure that Jeff will be kept well out of the way. Fortunately for both Jeff and Fay, the disgruntled Marty decides not to take Jeff at his word and refuses to leave him alone.

Screenplay: Donald James
Director: Leslie Norman

CAST
Joshua Crackan – Felix Aylmer
Fay Crackan – Liz Fraser
Rev. Henry Crackan – Neil McCallum
Mesmero – Dick Bentley
Hodder – Meredith Edwards
Johnny Crackan – John Hallam
Ramon – Earl Green
Sung Lee Crackan – John A. Tinn
Punter – Michael Ripper
Young stage director – Graham Armitage

Just like that! The amazing Mesmero subjects Fay to an uplifting experience.

23.
The Trouble
With Women
Friday, 20 February 1970: 7.30 pm

Jeff becomes embroiled in what seems a straightforward matrimonial dispute when blonde Susan Lang hires him to confirm that her husband Paul is having an affair. Marty is wary – he says he doesn't like the blonde's aura. But Jeff likes the £100 advance payment she has made.

What Susan has omitted to mention is that Paul Lang is the owner of a crooked gambling club and, in the course of his investigations when forced to play by Alan Corder, the club manager, Jeff not only loses his £100 fee at the tables but a couple of hundred more for good measure. He has just 24 hours in which to repay the debt. He does however have the satisfaction of confirming that Paul Lang is having an affair with

a striking brunette after spotting the two together at Ascot.

So Jeff's principal chore is to win back his money – quickly. He joins Lang in a poker game and, with Marty's invaluable help (there is nothing like an extra pair of eyes to tell you what cards your opponent is holding), he scoops the kitty, recouping his losses...and with substantial interest.

The case appears to be drifting towards a smooth conclusion until Susan telephones to say that her husband will be away for the day and that this will present an opportunity for Jeff to visit their home and obtain the evidence necessary to prove that Paul is a crook. But it is a trap, one into which Jeff obligingly falls. For while Jeff is at the house, the body of Paul Lang is discovered and, once again, he becomes a suspect for murder.

Demonstrating commendable caution, the police agree to allow Jeff time to clear his name before

Marty realises that Corder and Susan Lang are more than just good friends.

Marty gives Jeff a helping hand at poker.

arresting him. It is Marty who makes the crucial breakthrough when finding a wig which proves conclusively that Susan and 'the other woman' are really one and the same person. The blonde pose was for Jeff's benefit – the brunette girlfriend seen with Paul was his own wife. And now that Paul is dead, the way is clear for Susan and Corder to further their romance and take over the club – if they can pin the murder on Jeff.

When they realise that Jeff knows the truth, there is only one course of action open. He too must be murdered. Marty saves the day by visiting an old gothic mansion to attend a meeting of the British Spiritualist Society. He jumps the queue of ghosts waiting to deliver messages to the other side and succeeds in getting the police called before Jeff is shot.

Screenplay: Tony Williamson
Director: Cyril Frankel

CAST
Alan Corder – Paul Maxwell
Susan Lang – Denise Buckley
Paul Lang – Edward Brayshaw
Harry – Robert Russell
Brin – Nik Zaran
Mrs. Halloway – Gwen Nelson
Poker player – Arnold Diamond
Second player – Neil Arden
Inspector – Frederick Treves
First ghost – Howard Goorney
Second ghost – Harry Hutchinson
PC Russell – Keith Grenville

24.
Vendetta for a Dead Man
Friday, 27 February 1970: 7.30 pm

Almost a year after Marty Hopkirk was responsible for his arrest, hardened criminal Jansen escapes from the prison psychiatric ward in which he has been detained. His aim is to exact full vengeance on Marty, and he has timed it to take place on the precise anniversary of his arrest, down to the very minute.

Forcing his way into Jeff's apartment, Jansen refuses to believe Randall when he says that Marty is dead. But to prove it, Jeff produces papers confirming that Marty's widow Jean has inherited everything.

Not to be deprived, Jansen vows that Jean shall also inherit the brutal revenge intended for her late husband. Jeff tries to warn Jean but there is no reply. The police are notified and are waiting for her when she returns home after an evening out with a man named Emil Cavallo-Smith. Jean's blossoming relationship with Cavallo-Smith infuriates the jealous Marty who, even though he is supposed to be six feet under, still considers her to be married to him.

The police guard proves hopelessly inadequate against a determined woman like Jean who manages to slip her minders for another rendezvous with Emil. Love-struck and dreamy-eyed, she is by now convinced that Emil is about to propose marriage although she has not definitely decided what her answer will be. Jeff and Marty are worried that Emil may be in league with Jansen and so, while exploring every avenue to hunt down the fugitive, they also

7. Just for the Record

make it their business to find out as much as possible about Jeannie's suitor. Despite a grilling of former associate Sam Grimes, the quest for Jansen draws a blank but they do discover that Emil already has a wife, a fact which serves to anger Marty all the more.

On a trip to the funfair with Emil, Jean suffers a terrifying confrontation with Jansen in the hall of mirrors. It is only due to Marty's ability to crack glass that Jean manages to escape. Back under police protection, Jean would appear to be safe but Jansen is a devious customer and, after trapping Emil, forces him to telephone her to arrange a meeting at his apartment above the cold storage plant he owns. While Emil is imprisoned among the carcasses of pork in his own refrigerator, Jean, having again eluded her police escort, arrives to find herself alone with Jansen. The vicious Jansen bundles her off to the same nearby cliff edge where, a year earlier, he had been cornered by Marty.

Meanwhile Jeff and Marty reach the refrigeration plant where they find the captive Emil. He stubbornly refuses to reveal the whereabouts of Jean and Jansen so Marty tells Jeff to put him back in cold storage. Frozen in a state of suspended animation, Emil is so close to death that Marty is able to converse with him on equal terms. Threatened by Marty that unless he co-operates he will not return to life, Emil finally talks and the information he imparts convinces Marty that Jansen has taken Jean to the cliffs. Before setting off for the trip to the seaside, Marty socks his love rival...for daring to mess around with Jeannie.

Jansen demands to know Marty's whereabouts.

High up on the cliffs, Jansen holds Jean at knife-point, waiting the few minutes for the appointed hour of five past midnight, the exact time a year ago that her husband caused his downfall. Jansen tells her: 'I'm going to give you the same choice as your husband gave me...Not much of a choice is it? But that's all he gave me – down there or eight years in jail.'

Just then, Jeff arrives and seeing history about to repeat itself with the remaining member of the detective partnership, Jansen plunges to his death in the choppy waters below rather than face another spell in prison.

Screenplay: Donald James
Director: Cyril Frankel

CAST
Jansen – George Sewell
Emil Cavallo-Smith – Barrie Ingham
Mrs. Cavallo-Smith – Ann Castle
Sam Grimes – Timothy West
Fairground concessionaire – Ron Pember
Police Sgt. bodyguard – Richard Owens
Police Inspector – William Dysart
Police Sgt. in car – Harry Davies
Police driver – Colin Rix
Blonde girl in car – Sue Vaughan

Jeff traps Jansen on a cliff ledge.

25.
You Can Always Find a Fall Guy

Friday, 6 March 1970: 7.30 pm

Jeff finds an unexpected visitor at his flat.

Returning home after a night on the tiles, Jeff lurches into his flat one morning to be greeted by a vision which suggests he is still in a state of intoxication. For sitting there is a highly attractive nun. She explains that St. Ursula's Convent needs his help to prove that Douglas Kershaw, who has been hired as an accountant, has been embezzling £6,000 of convent funds. The sisters do not wish Kershaw to be sent to jail, she says – they just want their money back. She tells Jeff that he can collect the incriminating accounts from the convent that evening. With that, she leaves the flat, sheds her habit and roars off in a red sports car.

Jeff and Marty drive down to the convent near Winchester in Jeannie's Mini (Jeff's car being in the garage for repairs) and collect an envelope from the sister who is waiting in the driveway. She departs but just as Jeff and Marty are about to do likewise, the alarm sounds. Jeff just has time to throw the envelope into a clump of bushes before the Mini is surrounded by patrol men with guard dogs. Jeff is taken away by a security officer called Edwards.

Marty had been unsure of the so-called nun all along and now he is proved right since the building turns out to be the headquarters of Winchester Electronics Research Corporation rather than a convent. Philip Yateman, an executive of the organisation, accuses Jeff of trespassing. When Yateman finds a card bearing Kershaw's name and address in Jeff's possession, he is even more suspicious – Kershaw has been trading stolen information from WERC. Yateman demands the return of the papers and threatens to call in the police, at which Marty creates one of his famous whirlwinds, allowing Jeff to escape and retrieve the envelope. Out of snarling range of the dogs, Jeff opens the envelope and discovers that it contains nothing more than newspaper.

Receiving a visit from Edwards, claiming to have traced Jeff via his car, Randall explains that he has been conned. He attempts to throw some light on the case by calling on Kershaw at his houseboat moored on the Thames but Kershaw declares that this sort of thing happens all the time in the world of industrial espionage. There is always a risk of detection so there has to be fall guy. In this instance, Jeff is the fall guy.

By now, the police have a warrant for Jeff's arrest. Suspecting Edwards (who could not have identified Jeff's car since he was using Jeannie's Mini), Jeff heads back to WERC. There he recognises the personnel manager, Miss Holliday, in her red sports car as the nun that set him up in the first place. Another call on Kershaw is rudely interrupted by the arrival of Miss Holliday and Yateman who overpowers Randall with a deft demonstration of martial arts. Yateman reveals that within a day, he will have obtained all of the company's research, worth £500,000. He has Jeff locked in a basement strong room at WERC with the promise that he will be back to kill him in 24 hours.

In desperation, Jeff summons Marty whose ingenuity at finding ways of transmitting messages to the other side scales new heights when he conducts a tour of London hospitals to find any patient hovering on the brink of death. He strikes it lucky as a patient momentarily dies on the operating table. The man's ghost appears and Marty tells him that when he returns to the land of the living, he must telephone the police and tell them and Edwards to search WERC's basements. There is an anxious wait for the patient to regain consciousness but when he does, he immediately asks for a telephone and relays Marty's instructions. Miss Holliday and Yateman are arrested just as they are about to flee and Jeff shows his gratitude by sending the patient a basket of fruit. The man is puzzled – he knows nothing of Jeff or Marty.

Screenplay: Donald James
Director: Ray Austin

CAST
Miss Holliday – Juliet Harmer
Yateman – Patrick Barr
Edwards – Garfield Morgan
Douglas Kershaw – Jeremy Young
Surgeon – Tony Steedman
First detective – Clifford Earl
Patient – Edward Caddick
Receptionist – Ingrid Sylvester
Nurse – Maggie London
Anaesthetist – Michael Graham
Mechanic – John Walker

26.
The Smile Behind the Veil
Friday, 13 March 1970: 7.30 pm

Visiting his own grave while his devoted widow Jean places flowers on it, Marty stays behind to watch the funeral of a girl racing driver, Caroline Seaton. Among the mourners are her brother Donald and his wife Cynthia but Marty's suspicions are aroused when he spots that, for all her outward grieving, Cynthia is smiling behind her veil.

Marty immediately begins to wonder whether Caroline's death was really an accident. Could it have been murder? He tries to persuade Jeff to investigate but has to trick him into visiting Donald Seaton's country home. Once there, Jeff innocently reveals that he is a private detective whereupon he is overpowered by two thugs, Hooper and Grant, knocked unconscious and hurled from a bridge into the fast-flowing waters below. Jeff's body floats downsteam. He is so close to drowning that he momentarily materialises as a ghost, dressed all in white, and fixes Marty with a stern glare. Marty responds by attracting the attention of a fisherman who manages to pull Jeff to safety. Having completed the rescue, the angler reveals that he is Donald Seaton.

He tells Jeff that the other 'Seaton' has stolen his identity. He recalls how at the age of 18 he ended up in prison and fell out with his father, preferring to live in Australia until recently returning to Britain for a death-bed reunion with the old man. Alas, his father died before this could take place and now the imposter, backed by solicitor Brooks, is claiming the estate following the convenient death of Caroline.

The problem facing Jeff is to determine which of the two Seatons is genuine. The first Seaton's housekeeper, Mrs. Evans, is convinced that her employer is a fake and produces a newspaper cutting which puts her own life in danger. As the plot thickens, further

efforts are made to kill Jeff who on one occasion is saved only by the wrong man being murdered. Two facts do emerge, however – Cynthia is the real Mrs. Seaton and both she and the man purporting to be her husband are ruthless killers.

When Cynthia and the man who has returned from Australia come face to face, the truth is finally revealed. Cynthia and he have long been separated and the imposter has assumed his identity so that he and Cynthia can inherit the family fortune. Now that the secret is out, Jeff is in even greater peril, dangling at the bottom of a wishing well.

Knowing he must get Jeff out to thwart the dastardly plan, Marty spots a pair of hikers walking near the well. He blows off the man's bobble hat, directing it towards a sign pointing to the wishing well. Seeing the sign, the couple decide to try their luck.

'I wish I was a millionaire,' cries the man into the well.

'I wish I was out of this perishing well,' replies Jeff.

Muddy but unbowed, Jeff is freed in time to help the police arrest the cuplrits.

Screenplay: Gerald Kelsey
Director: Jeremy Summers

CAST
Seaton – Alex Scott
Cynthia – Hilary Tindall
Donald Seaton – Gary Watson
Mrs. Evans – Freda Jackson
Hooper – Peter Jesson
Grant – Robin Hawdon
Brooks – George Howe
Dyson – John Bott
Male hiker – Michael Radford
Girl hiker – Clare Jenkins
Police Constable – David Forbes
Policeman – Peter Lawrence

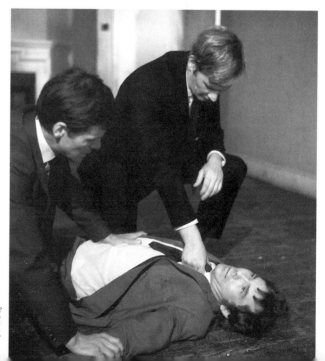

Jeff finds himself on the receiving end from hired thugs Grant and Hooper.

Devotees of the exploits of Jeff and Marty
can join the *Randall & Hopkirk (deceased)*
Appreciation Society whose address is:
10 Brooke Avenue
Edgware
Middlesex
HA8 9XF

CATCH RANDALL & HOPKIRK deceased APPEARING ON VIDEO

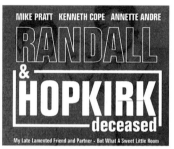

MIKE PRATT KENNETH COPE ANNETTE ANDRE

RANDALL & HOPKIRK deceased

My Late Lamented Friend and Partner • But What A Sweet Little Room

There's something different about this pair of private eyes ... one of them is dead!

VOLUME ONE PG

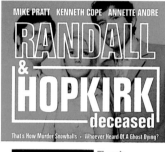

MIKE PRATT KENNETH COPE ANNETTE ANDRE

RANDALL & HOPKIRK deceased

That's How Murder Snowballs • Whoever Heard Of A Ghost Dying?

There's something different about this pair of private eyes ... one of them is dead!

VOLUME TWO PG

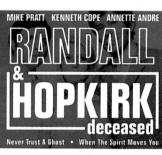

MIKE PRATT KENNETH COPE ANNETTE ANDRE

RANDALL & HOPKIRK deceased

Never Trust A Ghost • When The Spirit Moves You

There's something different about this pair of private eyes ... one of them is dead!

VOLUME THREE PG

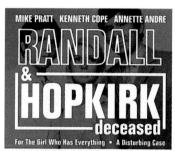

MIKE PRATT KENNETH COPE ANNETTE ANDRE

RANDALL & HOPKIRK deceased

For The Girl Who Has Everything • A Disturbing Case

There's something different about this pair of private eyes ... one of them is dead!

VOLUME FOUR PG

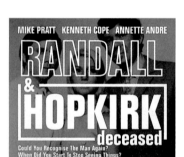
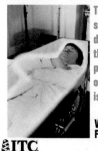

MIKE PRATT KENNETH COPE ANNETTE ANDRE

RANDALL & HOPKIRK deceased

Could You Recognise The Man Again? When Did You Start To Stop Seeing Things?

There's something different about this pair of private eyes ... one of them is dead!

VOLUME FIVE PG

MIKE PRATT KENNETH COPE ANNETTE ANDRE

RANDALL & HOPKIRK deceased

Murder Ain't What It Used To Be! • The House On Haunted Hill

There's something different about this pair of private eyes ... one of them is dead!

VOLUME SIX PG

MIKE PRATT KENNETH COPE ANNETTE ANDRE

RANDALL & HOPKIRK deceased

The Trouble With Women • Who Killed Cock Robin

There's something different about this pair of private eyes ... one of them is dead!

COMMEMORATIVE **25**th ANNIVERSARY EDITION

VOLUME SEVEN PG

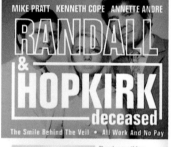

MIKE PRATT KENNETH COPE ANNETTE ANDRE

RANDALL & HOPKIRK deceased

The Smile Behind The Veil • All Work And No Pay

There's something different about this pair of private eyes ... one of them is dead!

COMMEMORATIVE **25**th ANNIVERSARY EDITION

VOLUME EIGHT PG

COMING SOON: VOLUMES 9-12

ITC